Favorite Party Dishes

Peaches and pears in brandy — a dessert for a special occasion

Mrs Beeton's Favorite Party Dishes

Edited by
Maggie Black

THE BOBBS-MERRILL COMPANY, INC.
Indianapolis • New York

We wish to thank Richard A. Ahrens and Arlene S. Bickel for their assistance in putting this book together.

Published by the Bobbs-Merrill Company, Inc.
Indianapolis   New York
ISBN 0-672-52321-3 Paperback
Library of Congress Catalog Card Number: 76-50467
Manufactured in the United States of America.
First U. S. printing.
Published under arrangement with Ottenheimer Publishers, Inc.

Contents

Weights and Measures Used in This Book

Liquid measures

60 drops	1 teaspoon
3 teaspoons	1 tablespoon
4 tablespoons	¼ cup
1 cup	½ pint
2 cups	1 pint
2 pints	1 quart
4 quarts	1 gallon

Spoons are standard teaspoons and tablespoons, which hold the amounts of liquid given above. They are measured with the contents leveled off, i.e. all spoonfuls are level spoonfuls.

The cup is a standard measuring cup that holds 8 fluid oz. or ½ pint.

Flour, sifted	4 tablespoons	1 oz.
Granulated sugar	2 tablespoons	1 oz.
Confectioners' sugar, sifted	3 tablespoons	1 oz.
Butter or margarine	2 tablespoons	1 oz.
Cornstarch	2 tablespoons	½ oz.
Granulated or powdered gelatin	3 tablespoons	1 oz.
Corn syrup	1 tablespoon	1 oz.
Flour, sifted	1 cup	4 oz.
Granulated sugar	1 cup	8 oz.
Confectioners' sugar, sifted	1 cup	3½ oz.
Butter or margarine	1 cup	8 oz.
Cornstarch	1 cup	4½ oz.
Corn syrup	1 cup	1 lb.
Cheese, cream	1 cup	8 oz.
Cheese, grated	4 cups	1 lb.

Precise metric equivalents are not very useful. The weights are almost impossible to measure accurately and are not used in ordinary cooking. Schools use a 25-gram unit for 1 oz. and for retested recipes. This means that they can use existing equipment. For instance, a 6-inch sandwich tin can be used for a 15-cm one, and a 7-inch tin for an 18-cm one. Yorkshire pudding using 100 grams flour fits into a 2 × 14 cm (8 in. × 5½ in.) baking tin.

Mrs. Beeton's recipes are all being retested so that they can be converted to metric measures when these come into general use.

Oven temperatures

	Fahrenheit	Celsius
Very cool	225 °F	110 °C
Very cool	250 °F	130 °C
Very cool	275 °F	140 °C
Cool	300 °F	150 °C
Warm	325 °F	170 °C
Moderate	350 °F	180 °C
Fairly hot	375 °F	190 °C
Fairly hot	400 °F	200 °C
Hot	425 °F	220 °C
Very hot	450 °F	230 °C
Very hot	475 °F	240 °C

Deep-fat frying table

Food	Bread Browns In	Fat Temp	Oil Temp
Uncooked mixtures, e.g. fritters	1 minute	370–375 °F	375–385 °F
Cooked mixtures, e.g. fish cakes	40 seconds	380–385 °F	385 °F
Fish	1 minute	375 °F	375 °F
French fries, potato straws, chips, etc.	20 seconds	390 °F	395 °F

Introduction

Most people have to give parties from time to time.

Within a family, for instance, traditional festivals such as Christmas and Easter usually call for some kind of family gathering, which often includes friends as well. So do children's birthdays. A wedding is nearly always celebrated with a party of some kind.

Other personal and family occasions that are often marked by a party include a 21st birthday, an engagement, and a silver wedding anniversary. Many people, too, like to commemorate an occasion such as moving into a new home by giving a party.

We give many other kinds of parties as well, which are not linked to special occasions. Many people need to give cocktail, lunch, or dinner parties at home for business reasons. Others give them just to bring friends together, or to return the hospitality of others. It may also be convenient to give guests a meal at home before taking them to the theater, or afterward. Young people especially sometimes like to have their friends around on a Sunday morning for brunch or lunch, to swim or play tennis. More formally, older people may well invite others to talk business over lunch; or they may meet for a club lunch, or just a social one. A willing hostess may also find herself giving various other kinds of parties for a club or society, from a fund-raising "coffee morning" to evening refreshments after a lecture.

Then, besides all these "parties for a reason," there are many parties that people give just because they like doing it: pancake parties, wine and cheese parties, beer and sausage parties, TV parties, and a great many others.

This book is designed to help any party-giver with ideas and recipes for many and various occasions, whether it means feeding more people than usual with easy dishes to do "for a crowd" or providing guests with more elaborate or formal dishes than in an everyday meal. Since every hostess secretly hopes to impress her guests, these dishes are designed to make a memorable meal.

The overall idea behind all the recipes and menus is to make the hostess' task easy. A gay, confident hostess creates the right atmosphere for a good party. A tired or harassed one often fails. This book aims to make party-giving pleasant and simple, so the hostess enjoys her own party and provides an enjoyable occasion.

Ideas for Special Occasions

AVOCADO PEARS AND SHRIMPS

2 large avocados	1¼ cups
2 tbs. olive	shelled shrimp
oil	Crisp lettuce
2 tbs. vinegar	leaves
Good pinch	Lemon
of salt	Pinch of sugar
Good pinch of	(optional)
pepper	¼ crushed clove
A little prepared	of garlic
mustard	(optional)

Halve the avocados. Blend the oil, vinegar, and seasonings together. Toss the shrimps in this, and then spoon into the avocado halves. Put onto crisp lettuce leaves and garnish with wedges of lemon.

A pinch of sugar can be added to the dressing if wished, also a little garlic.

4 servings

ASPARAGUS "AU NATUREL"

1 bundle of	¼ cup butter
asparagus	Lemon juice
Salt	

Trim the hard white ends of the asparagus to lengths suitable for serving. Scrape the stalks with a sharp knife, working downward from the head. Wash them well in cold water. Tie them into small bundles with the heads in one direction. Retrim the stalks evenly. Keep them in cold water until ready to cook. Cook very gently, with the heads away from source of heat, in just enough salted boiling water to cover. When tender (in about 15-20 min.), drain and serve. Serve with melted butter, seasoned and lightly flavored with lemon.

Note: To ensure that the tender point of the asparagus is not overcooked by the time the stem is ready, thin asparagus should be cooked "standing." This can be achieved in an "asparagus boiler," a narrow, very deep pan. A bottling jar half-filled with boiling water, stood in a deep saucepan of boiling water, serves as a very good substitute. The asparagus is placed stems down in the jar, and the points cook more slowly in steam only. Allow 30 min. for this method of cooking.

Allow 6 or 8 medium stalks per person

GLOBE ARTICHOKES WITH HOLLANDAISE SAUCE

6 globe artichokes	1¼ cups Hollandaise
Salt	Sauce *or*
1 tbs. lemon	¼ cup melted
juice	butter

1

Asparagus "au Naturel"

ally until all is absorbed. Season, add lemon juice to taste, and serve immediately.

STUFFED ARTICHOKE BOTTOMS

Artichoke bottoms	1 tbs. stuffing
Butter *or*	for each
margarine	(approx.)

Where economy does not matter, globe artichokes may be cooked as in the preceding recipe and only the bottoms or "fonds" used. After cooking, the leaves are carefully pulled out of the artichokes so that the bottoms are retained unbroken.

Stuffings
1) Cooked rice, well seasoned and flavored with cheese, preferably Parmesan.

2) Fried finely chopped shallot, young cooked peas, mint, and seasoning.

3) Cooked sausage meat, chopped chives, and French mustard.

4) Finely chopped fried onion, mushroom, and a little tomato puree.

Toss the cooked artichoke bottoms in hot butter or margarine. Pile the hot, well-flavored stuffing on each bottom. Serve immediately. Allow 1 artichoke bottom per person.

Cooking time 5 – 7 min. to fry the bottoms

CONSOMMÉ MADRILENE

5 cups brown	1 bay leaf
stock	¼-½ lb. lean
1 lb. tomatoes	beef
1 green pepper	1 carrot
1 clove of garlic	1 egg white
Parsley stalks	1 onion
Thyme	1 stick of celery

Cut up the tomatoes and green pepper. Tie the herbs together in a small piece of muslin. Shred and soak the beef in ¼ pt. water. Beat the egg white slightly. Put all ingredients into a pan and simmer very gently for 1 hr. Strain as usual. To garnish, cut tiny dice from the firm flesh of skinned tomato. Serve the consommé hot or iced; if iced, it should be almost liquid and may therefore need a little beating.

6 servings

Soak the artichokes in cold salted water for at least 1 hr., to ensure the removal of all dust and insects. Wash them well. Cut off the tails and trim the bottoms with a sharp knife. Cut off the outer leaves and trim the tops of the rest with scissors. Put them into a pan with just enough boiling water to cover them, adding salt and the lemon juice. Cook until tender, 15-45 min., according to size and freshness (when cooked leaves pull out easily). Test frequently after 15 min., as they are apt to break and become discolored if overcooked. Remove from water and drain them well by turning them upside down. Serve with Hollandaise Sauce or melted butter.

HOLLANDAISE SAUCE

2 tbs. wine	¼-½ cup butter
vinegar	Salt and pepper
2 egg yolks	Lemon juice

Boil the vinegar until it is reduced by half; allow to cool. Mix the cool vinegar with the egg yolks in a bowl and place this over hot water. Beat the egg yolks until they begin to thicken, then beat in the butter gradu-

DEVILED LOBSTER

1 boiled lobster	Cayenne pepper
Butter	A few browned
3 tbs. white	bread crumbs
bread crumbs	
2 tbs. white	
sauce *or* cream	

Cut the lobster in two lengthwise; remove the meat carefully, as the half shell must be kept whole; chop the meat finely. Melt 3 tbs. butter and pour it on the lobster. Add the white bread crumbs and the sauce, season rather highly with cayenne, and mix well. Press the mixture lightly into the shells, cover with browned bread crumbs, put 3 or 4 pieces of butter on top, and bake for about 20 min. in a moderate oven (180 °C, 350 °F). Serve hot or cold.

2 servings

Globe Artichokes

LOBSTER THERMIDOR

2 small boiled	1 level tsp.
lobsters	prepared mustard
1 shallot	Pinch of cayenne
½ cup white	pepper
wine	A little grated
3 tbs. butter	cheese
⅝ cup Béchamel	Parsley to
Sauce	garnish

Cut the lobsters in half lengthwise and remove the stomach and the intestinal cord. Remove the meat from the shell and cut into slices, keeping the knife slanted. Chop the shallot very finely. Put the white wine in a small saucepan and cook the shallot until it is tender and the wine is reduced to half. Meanwhile, melt the butter and heat the meat very carefully in this. Add the shallot and wine mixture to the lobster meat with the sauce, mustard, and pepper; mix; return to the shells. Sprinkle with grated cheese and brown under a hot broiler. Serve garnished with parsley and accompanied by a simple salad or plain lettuce.

4 servings

CHATEAUBRIAND STEAK

A double filet	Olive oil *or*
steak not less	melted butter
than 1½ in.	Salt and pepper
thick	

Wipe the steak. Remove any sinew or skin. Cover the meat with a cloth and beat lightly to flatten. Brush with oil or melted butter, and season. Place under a hot broiler and cook both sides quickly; the steak should be well-browned but slightly underdone. Serve immediately on a hot dish with Potato Sticks or new potatoes. Serve also Maitre d'Hôtel Butter and gravy, or Demi-Glacé, Tomato, or Béchamel Sauce.

TOURNEDOS OF BEEF, ROSSINI

1½ lb. filet	1 tbs. brown
of beef, cut as	sauce
tournedos	Salt and pepper
¼ lb. chicken	1 tbs. olive
livers	oil
¼ cup butter *or*	Meat glaze
fat	Croutes of fried
1 shallot	bread
3 tbs. foie gras	1¼-2 cups Demi-
or pâté	Glacé Sauce

3

Wipe the beef and cut into rounds 2½-in. diameter and ½-in. thick; that is, cut as tournedos. Wash, dry, and slice the livers. Melt 2 tbs. of the fat in a sauté pan and fry the finely chopped shallot slightly. Add the liver, and sauté for a few minutes. Drain off the fat and pound the livers with the foie gras or pâté, brown sauce, and seasoning until smooth, then pass this through a wire sieve. Heat the remainder of the fat with the olive oil and fry the tournedos quickly until browned on both sides. Drain and cover one side of each with the liver stuffing. Brush with meat glaze, place on the fried croutes, and put in the oven to become thoroughly hot. Arrange the filets on a hot dish and serve the Demi-Glacé Sauce separately.

6 servings

CROWN ROAST OF LAMB WITH SAFFRON RICE

A 2-section crown roast of lamb Oil for brushing	Salt Pepper

Stuffing:

2 tbs. butter	2 oz. frozen peas
1 stick celery, chopped	3 tbs. chopped, blanched
1 onion, chopped	almonds
¾ cup long-grain white rice	2 dessert apples, cored and diced
5 tbs. dry white wine	2 tbs. butter
2½ cups chicken stock, heated, with a scant ¼ tsp. powdered saffron	

Ask the butcher to prepare the crown roast. Place the roast in a roasting pan. Brush with oil and season well with salt and pepper. Wrap a small piece of foil around the top of each rib to prevent it from scorching during cooking. Cook at 190 °C, 375 °F, for 1¼-1½ hr. Approx. 30 min. before the roast is finished cooking, prepare the saffron rice stuffing by melting the butter in a saucepan and cooking the celery and onion until soft but not

browned. Stir in the raw rice and cook for 1-2 min. Pour on the wine and cook gently until the rice has absorbed it. Add 1¼ cups of the saffron-flavored chicken stock and cook, uncovered, stirring occasionally, until almost all the liquid is absorbed. Pour the remaining stock over the rice and cook until it has been completely absorbed and the rice is just tender. Remove from the heat and add the peas, chopped nuts, diced apple, and butter and cover the saucepan with a tight-fitting lid.

Drain the roast and place on a warmed serving dish. Remove the foil from the rib bones. Fill the roast with the hot saffron rice. Top each rib with a cutlet frill and serve. (Any extra rice can be served separately.)

6 – 8 servings

SCALLOPS EN BROCHETTE

4 large scallops	4 thick slices
1 cup rice	pineapple
8 small strips bacon	

Scallops are usually opened at the fish market and displayed in their flat shells. If the scallops are to be served in their shells, ask for the *deep* shells. If, however, it is necessary to open scallops, they should be put over a gentle heat to allow the shells to open. When they have opened, remove from the shells, trim away the beard, and remove the black parts. Wash the scallops well, drain, and dry. Wash and dry the shells; keep the deep shells for serving dishes. Scallops are in season from November to March. They can be served baked, fried, poached, or broiled as follows: Cook the rice in fast-boiling salted water until just tender. Wash the scallops and cut in half, then roll each half in a strip of bacon. Impale on a thin skewer with a half slice of pineapple between each. Broil under moderate heat, turning once, for 8-10 min. Drain the rice when cooked, rinse under cold running water, then spread out on a sieve and reheat. Pile up on a dish and lay the 4 skewers on the rice. Serve hot.

4 servings

GRAY MULLET OR TROUT EN PAPILLOTES

4 gray mullet or trout	1 tbs. lemon juice
Salt and pepper	

Prepare the fish, sprinkle the insides with salt and pepper, and wrap carefully in aluminum foil, twisting the ends securely. Place on a baking sheet and bake for about 15-20 min. in a fairly hot oven (190°C, 375°F). When cooked, loosen the foil carefully and place the fish on a hot dish. Add the lemon juice to the liquid that has collected in the paper, pour this over the fish, and serve. Garnish with slices of lemon and sprigs of parsley.

If liked, the mullet or trout may be stuffed with a mixture of ½ cup fresh bread crumbs, 1 level tbs. grated onion, 2 level tsp. chopped parsley, salt and pepper to taste, moistened with a little milk. Allow a little longer cooking time.

4 servings

TROUT "AU BLEU"

1 6–8-oz. trout	Salt
Vinegar	Parsley

The essential factor of this famous dish is that the trout should be alive until just before cooking. In restaurants they are often kept in a tank from which the customer selects his fish. The fish should be stunned, cleaned (gutted), and immediately plunged into a pan of boiling salted water to which a little vinegar has been added. (The fish are not scaled or washed, as this would spoil the blue color.) Draw the pan aside, or reduce the heat, and poach the fish for about 10-12 min. Drain, and serve garnished with parsley and accompanied by melted butter, Hollandaise Sauce, and small boiled potatoes.

LOBSTERS — HOW TO CHOOSE

Lobsters can be obtained all year, but are scarce from December to March. They are cheapest during the summer months. Lobsters are usually bought already boiled, but live lobsters can be obtained to order if a few days' notice is given to the fish market. Choose one of medium size and heavy in weight. If fresh, the tail of a cooked lobster will be stiff; if gently raised, it will return with a spring. The narrowness of the back part of the tail and the stiffness of the two uppermost fins (swimmerettes) in the tail distinguish the cock lobster from the hen.

BOILING A LOBSTER

There are two methods of boiling lobsters, each method having points in its favor.

Method I

Wash the lobster well before boiling; tie the claws securely. Have ready a saucepan of boiling water, salted in the proportion of ¼ lb. salt to 1 gal. water. Throw the lobster head first into the water (this instantly destroys life), keep it boiling for 20-45 min., according to size, and skim well. Allow 20 min.-½ hr. for small lobsters and ½-¾ hr. for large lobsters. If boiled too long, the meat becomes thready; if not done enough, the coral is not red. If serving in the shell, rub the shells with a little salad oil to brighten the color.

Method 2

Put the lobsters into warm water, bring the water gradually to a boil, and boil as above. Many believe this to be a more humane method of killing, as the lobster is lulled to sleep and does not realize it is being killed.

PREPARING A LOBSTER FOR EATING

Wipe the lobster well with a clean damp cloth and twist off claws and legs. Place lobster on a board parallel to the edge, with back uppermost and head to the left. Cut along the center of back, from junction of head with body to tail, using a sharp, stainless knife. Reverse so that tail is to left, and cut along head; the stomach, which lies just behind the mouth, is not cut until last. Remove intestinal cord, remove stomach and coral (if any) and keep for garnish. The meat may be left in the shell or removed and used as required. To remove the meat, knock tips of the claws with the back of a knife and drain away

Preparing Trout en Papillotes

Chateaubriand Steak

any water. Tap sharply around the broadest part of each claw, and the shell should fall apart. Cut the cartilage between pincers, open the pincers, and the meat can be removed in one piece. Remove the meat from the smaller joints of claws.

SALMI OF PHEASANT

1 pheasant	½ cup Madeira
¼ cup butter	(optional)
¼ tsp. grated	6-8 slices goose
lemon rind	liver *or* pâté
2 shallots	6-8 mushrooms
¼ tsp. thyme	Salt and pepper
1 bay leaf	
1¼ cups brown	
sauce	

Garnish:
Croutes of fried bread (triangular) *or*
Fleurons of Puff Pastry

Pluck, draw, and truss bird for roasting. Baste it well with hot butter; roast in a hot oven (220-230 °C, 425-450 °F) for 30 min., basting frequently. Pour the butter used for basting into a saucepan, add grated lemon rind, chopped shallots, thyme, and bay leaf. Cut up the bird; lay aside breast, wings, and legs; cut remainder into neat pieces, add these to the saucepan and fry. If any fat remains, pour it from the saucepan, put in the brown sauce, wine (if used), and season. Simmer for 10 min. Add remainder of pheasant; heat thoroughly. Meanwhile, reheat the butter, fry in it the slices of goose liver, if used, and the mushrooms. Correct seasoning of sauce. Serve pheasant with pâté

Crown Roast of Lamb with Saffron Rice

or liver; strain the sauce over; garnish with
the Croutes or Fleurons and the mushrooms.

4- 5 servings   Cooking time – about 1 ¼ hr.
in all

GROUSE PIE

2 grouse	1¼ cups good
¾ lb. rump steak	stock
2-3 slices of	Puff Pastry,
bacon	frozen *or* using
2 hard-boiled	2 cups flour,
eggs	etc.
Salt and pepper	

Cut up the birds, and discard vent-end
parts of the backs, as these will impart a
bitter flavor to the pie. Slice the steak
thinly, slice eggs, and cut the bacon into
strips. Line the bottom of a pie dish with
pieces of seasoned meat, cover with a
layer of grouse, add some bacon, egg, and
seasoning. Repeat until dish is full. Add
sufficient stock to ¾ fill the pie dish, cover
with Puff Pastry as above and bake for
1½-1¾ hr. for the first 15 min. of this time,
have the oven hot (220-230 °C, 425-450 °F),
then lower the heat to moderate (180-190
°C, 350-375 °F) and cover the pastry with
aluminum foil so that the filling can cook

7

another 1¼-1½ hr. Glaze the pie ½ hr. before cooking is complete. Simmer the necks and trimmings of the birds in the remaining stock, strain, season, and pour into the pie before serving. Finely chopped mushrooms, parsley, and shallots may be added to the pie, if liked.

6 - 8 servings   Cooking time – 1¾ hr.

ARTICHOKE BOTTOMS
WITH BÉCHAMEL SAUCE

6 artichoke bottoms	1¼ cups Béchamel Sauce
¼ cup butter *or* margarine	

Trim the cooked artichoke bottoms and, if large, cut in halves. Toss in hot butter or margarine. Season and serve with hot Béchamel Sauce.

4 - 6 servings   Cooking time – 7 min. to fry the bottoms

STEAMED CUCUMBER
WITH WHITE SAUCE

2 large cucumbers	2 cups white sauce
2 tbs. butter *or* margarine	1 egg
1 tsp. finely chopped shallot	1 tsp. finely chopped parsley
	Salt and pepper

Peel the cucumber and steam it until tender (about 20 min.). Drain well and cut into 1-in. slices. Melt the butter in a saucepan, put in the shallot, and cook it without browning. Add the sliced cucumber, toss over heat for a few minutes, then stir in the white sauce. Just before boiling point is reached, add the well-beaten egg and parsley, stir, and cook gently until the egg thickens. Season and serve hot.

6 servings

GREEN PEAS, FRENCH STYLE

2 lb. green peas (3¾ cups shelled peas)	¼ cup butter *or* margarine
4 very small onions *or* spring onions	2 tsp. sugar
	Salt and pepper
1 head lettuce	Egg yolk (optional)

Shell the peas. Peel the onions. Remove the outer leaves of the lettuce; wash the heart, leaving it whole. Put the peas into a saucepan, add the lettuce heart, onions, and the butter cut into small pieces. Stir in the sugar and a little salt. Cover with the lid and cook over a very low heat, about 1 hr., shaking the pan occasionally. Re-season and serve. The liquid in the pan may be thickened with an egg yolk before serving.

6 servings

POACHED SPINACH

3 lb. spinach	2 tbs. cream (optional)
2 tbs. butter *or* margarine	Salt and pepper

Pick over the spinach carefully and wash it at least 3 times. Break off the stalks and at the same time pull off the central ribs if coarse. (Young, summer spinach need not be stripped of the central ribs.) Put the wet leaves into a saucepan, without additional water. Cook slowly until tender, about 15 min., stirring the spinach in the pan occasionally. The pan should have a tightly fitting lid. Drain well, pressing out the water. Reheat in the butter. Add the cream, if used, and mix it well with the spinach. Season, and serve hot.

For spinach puree, drain the cooked spinach well and sieve it or puree in an electric blender before adding the cream.

5 - 6 servings

POTATOES ANNA

2 lb. even-sized potatoes	Melted clarified butter *or* margarine
Salt and pepper	

Grease a thick cake pan and line the bottom with greased paper. Peel and trim the potatoes so that they will give equal-sized slices. Slice them very finely and arrange a layer of slightly overlapping slices. Sprinkle with fat and seasoning. Make a second layer of potatoes and repeat. Continue until the pan is full, pressing each layer well into the pan. Cover with a lid and bake in a fairly hot oven (190 °C, 375 °F) for about 1 hr. Look at the potatoes from time to time and add more butter if they become dry. Turn out onto a hot dish and serve at once.

6 servings   Cooking time – about 1 hr.

SAUTÉED POTATOES

6 medium potatoes	2-4 tbs. butter or margarine Seasoning

Cook the potatoes, preferably in their skins, until just soft. Let them dry thoroughly, then peel and slice them ¼ in. thick. Heat the fat in a frying pan and put in the potatoes. Season them with salt and pepper. Toss in the fat until they are light brown and have absorbed all the fat. Serve at once.

4 - 6 servings

ENGLISH POTATO CHIPS AND POTATO STRAWS

6 medium potatoes	Deep fat Salt

Scrub and rinse the potatoes. Peel them thinly. For chips-cut into sticks about 2 in. long and ½ in. wide and thick. For french fries, cut into strips about 3 in. long and ¼ in. wide and thick. Drop them into cold water as they are cut. Rinse and drain them and dry them in a clean cloth. Put them into the frying basket and lower them gently into hot deep fat at 180 °C, 360 °F. (Keep the heat fairly high, as the potatoes will have cooled the fat.) When the potatoes are soft but *not* brown — about 3 min. for chips and 1 min. for straws — lift out the basket and heat the fat to 190 °C, 375 °F. Put back the basket and leave in the fat until the potatoes are crisp and golden brown — about 3 min. for chips and 2 min. for straws. Drain on absorbent paper, sprinkle with salt and serve immediately.

Note: If potato chips or straws are to be served with fried fish or any other fried dish, the second frying of the potatoes to brown and crisp them should be done after the fish, etc., is fried. In this way the potatoes will be sent to the table in their best condition.

6 servings   Cooking time – for chips, about 6 min.; for straws, about 3 min.

MILANAISE SOUFFLÉ

2 lemons	1½ tbs. gelatin
3-4 eggs, according to size	⅝ cup water
	1¼ cups heavy
⅝ cup sugar	cream

Decoration:
Chopped pistachio nuts

Wash lemons, dry, and grate rind finely. Beat the egg yolks, sugar, rind, and lemon juice over hot water until thick and creamy, then remove bowl from the hot water and continue beating until cool. Soften the gelatin in the ¼ pt. water, and heat to dissolve. Half beat the cream. Beat the egg whites very stiffly. Add the gelatin, still hot, in a thin stream, to the egg mixture, and stir in as you do it. Fold in the cream and the stiffly beaten egg whites. Fold the mixture very lightly until setting is imminent, when the mixture pulls against the spoon. Pour into a soufflé dish and leave to set. Remove the paper band by coaxing it away from the mixture with a knife dipped in hot water. Decorate the sides with chopped, blanched pistachio nuts, and the top with whipped cream, if liked.

This is a good "basic" soufflé recipe. It can be flavored and decorated with almost any flavoring and garnish, such as coffee, chocolate, fruit, or a liqueur, with appropriate small sweets or nuts as decoration.

6 servings   Setting time – 2 hr.

Note: Tie a double band of paper around a 1-pt. china soufflé dish, so that 3 in. of the paper extends above the rim. This makes a mold in which the soufflé mixture will set 1-1½ in. above the rim and, on removal of the paper, will appear to have "risen" above the dish.

Salmi of Pheasant with Croûtes

Sautéed Potatoes

HAWAIIAN DREAMS

1 large can crushed pineapple	³⁄₈ cup chopped toasted almonds
1½ tbs. gelatin	⁵⁄₈ cup sweetened whipped cream
2 tsp. lemon juice	6-8 maraschino cherries
1 pt. vanilla *or* chocolate ice cream	

Measure the crushed pineapple and make it up to 2½ cups with water. Dissolve the gelatin in a little of the liquid but do not allow to boil. Add it to the crushed pineapple with the lemon juice. Pour into individual glasses to set. Just before serving, place a scoop of ice cream on top of the

Milanaise Soufflé

Hawaiian Dreams

set mixture. Sprinkle with nuts. Decorate with a rose of cream and place a cherry on top.

6 individual glasses

PAVLOVA CAKE

3 egg whites	**½ tsp. cornstarch**
¾ cup sugar	**½ tsp. vinegar**
½ tsp. vanilla extract	**Filling as below**

Beat the egg whites until stiff. Continue beating, gradually adding the sugar. Beat until sugar is dissolved; at this stage the mixture should be very stiff and standing well in peaks. Fold in vanilla, cornstarch and vinegar. Spread mixture in a 6-8 in. circle on greaseproof paper on a baking sheet, making the sides higher than the center, to form a shell to hold filling. Place in a cool oven at 150 °C, 300 °F, for 1-1½ hr.

The Pavlova should be crisp and very lightly tinted on the surface yet remain soft and of the consistency of marshmallow in the center. Cool, and remove very carefully onto a flat cake tray or board. Fill, and serve cut in wedges.

Filling:
Pile 1¼ cups whipped and flavored cream into the Pavlova shell; on top of this arrange a selection of fruit: pineapple, strawberries or other berry fruits, cherries, apricots, mandarins, passion fruit, grapes, fresh or canned peaches, etc., according to taste, and season. Finally, decorate with angelica, maraschino cherries, or almonds as desired.

There are many other Pavlova filling mixtures. Try black currants with a little cassis liqueur, or pear slices and raspberries with lemon juice.

Note: You can also decorate the shell in various ways. Use a fancy pastry bag to make small rosettes on the sides, for instance.

11

CREPES SUZETTE

1¼ cups pancake batter	Confectioners' sugar
	Brandy *or* rum
Filling:	
¼ cup butter	1 tsp. lemon juice
⅜ cup sugar	
Grated rind of ½ orange	1 tbs. kirsch *or* curaçao
2 tsp. orange juice	

Make the batter and leave it to stand. Cream together the butter and sugar for the filling until very soft. Then work in the orange juice, rind, lemon juice, and liqueur. Make a very thin pancake, spread with some filling, roll up, and dredge with confectioners' sugar. Put into a warm place while making and filling the rest of the pancakes. Just before serving, pour the warmed brandy or rum over the pancakes and light it. Serve immediately.

If you prefer, warm the filling with the brandy until liquid and pour it over the unfilled pancakes folded over twice. Light and serve.

PEACHES PRESERVED IN BRANDY

Peaches	Water
Sugar	Brandy

Dip peaches in hot water, one at a time, and rub off the "fuzz" with a clean towel. Weigh. For each lb. fruit allow ¾ lb. sugar and 8 oz. water. Boil the sugar and water together for 10 min. without stirring. Add the peaches to the syrup and cook (only a few at a time to prevent bruising) for about 5 min., until tender. Remove the peaches from the syrup with a strainer and pack firmly into hot sterilized jars. Continue cooking the syrup, after removing peaches, until thick. Cool and measure. Add equal quantity of brandy. Bring to boiling point and fill jars of peaches to overflowing. Seal.
The following sweets can be served with coffee:

PEPPERMINT CREAMS

1 lb. confectioners' sugar	1-2 drops oil of peppermint *or* 2 tsp. peppermint extract
Whites of 2 large eggs	

Sift the confectioners' sugar and add the stiffly beaten egg whites and the peppermint flavoring. A very little green color may be added if liked. Mix all well together to a firm dough-like ball and roll out, well-sifted with confectioners' sugar, to about ¼-⅛ in. thick. Cut out with a small round sweet cutter and leave on a wire tray to dry out for 12 hr. Pack into an airtight container. The creams may be coated with melted chocolate if desired. For this, dissolve some broken chocolate in a bowl over hot water and dip the creams into the chocolate, holding them on a fine skewer or a sweet-dipping fork. Decorate with crystallized rose or violet petals, sugar mimosa, or flaked almonds. Allow to set on clean waxed paper before serving.

Dates
Dates can be served plain or stuffed. To stuff: slit the date and remove the stone. Fill the cavity with a whole blanched almond or roll of Marzipan. Roll in granulated sugar.

MARZIPAN

1 lb. confectioners' sugar	2 egg whites
1 cup water	1 cup sifted sugar
2¼ cups ground almonds	Flavoring

Boil the sugar and water to 240 °F, then draw the sugar boiler or pan aside, and, when the syrup has cooled slightly, add the almonds and egg whites. Stir over a low heat for a few minutes, then turn onto a shallow pan, stir in the confectioners' sugar, and work with a spatula until cool enough to handle. Knead with the hands until perfectly smooth; add flavoring and coloring. Mold into small balls and press half a walnut into each, or shape as miniature fruit, etc.

Dishes for Dinner Parties

GRAPEFRUIT BASKETS

½ grapefruit per person	Sugar to taste
1 wedge fresh melon per person	1 sprig fresh mint per person
4-6 pineapple chunks per person (fresh or canned)	4-6 fresh orange segments per person
	3 maraschino cherries per person

Halve each grapefruit. Remove and skin the sections. Discard core and seeds. Mix the skinned sections with diced melon, pineapple, and skinned section of fresh orange. Add halved maraschino cherries. Flavor with sugar to taste, but do not make too sweet. Replace the fruit in the grapefruit skins. Chill. When ready to serve, top each grapefruit half with a sprig of mint. Serve in individual bowls or champagne glasses.

SHRIMP COCKTAIL

Heart of small lettuce head	1 tsp. tarragon vinegar
10 oz. shrimps	Good pinch of salt
5 tbs. mayonnaise	Good pinch of cayenne pepper
1 tsp. chili vinegar, if available	Lemon

Dressed Crab

DRESSED CRAB

One 2½-3 lb. crab	A little lemon
Salt and pepper	juice (optional)
Fresh bread	French Dressing
crumbs	
(optional)	

Garnish:

1 hard-boiled egg	Parsley

Pick the crab meat from the shells. Mix the dark crab meat with salt and pepper, fresh bread crumbs, and a little lemon juice if liked. The bread crumbs are optional, but they lessen the richness and give a firmer texture. Press the mixture lightly against the sides of the previously cleaned shell. Flake up the white meat, mix with French Dressing, and pile in the center of the shell. Garnish with sieved egg yolk, chopped egg white, chopped parsley, sieved coral if any, and decorate with small claws. Make a necklace with the small claws, place on a dish, and rest the crab on this. Surround with salad.

4 servings

1 tbs. tomato
 puree (*see* **below**) *or*
 tomato ketchup

Wash and dry the lettuce very well — pick out the tiny leaves and break into very small pieces. Arrange in cocktail glasses. Put the shrimps on top. Mix the mayonnaise with the tomato ketchup or puree — to obtain this, rub one large tomato through a fine sieve. Add the vinegars and seasoning. Put the shrimps on top and garnish with a piece of lemon and a dusting of cayenne pepper. Serve very cold.

4 servings

POTTED SHRIMPS

2½ cups shrimps —	Pinch of salt
measure when	Grating of
shelled	nutmeg
¼-⅜ cup butter	Lettuce
Good pinch of	Lemon
cayenne pepper	

Heat the butter and turn the shrimps in this until they are well coated, but do not cook them. Add the seasonings and nutmeg. Pour into small molds or dishes and leave until the butter is set. Turn out onto a bed of crisp lettuce and garnish with lemon. Serve with cayenne pepper and crisp toast.

CUCUMBER CREAM SOUP

1 lb. cucumber	Lemon juice
2 tbs. butter	Green food
6 spring onions	coloring
¼ cup flour	A sprig of mint
2½ cups white	A sprig of parsley
stock	5 tbs. cream
Salt and pepper	

Peel the cucumber; reserve a 2-in. length for garnish; slice the rest. Melt the butter in a deep pan and cook the onions gently, without browning, for 10 min. Stir in the flour, then the stock, and bring to boiling point. Add the sliced cucumber and cook until tender. Sieve through a nylon sieve. Season, and add lemon juice to taste. Cut the 2-in. piece of cucumber into ¼-in. cubes and boil these in a little stock or water until just tender, then add them to the finished soup. Five minutes before serving the soup add the mint and parsley. Tint the soup pale green. Stir the cream into the hot soup immediately before serving.

4 servings *Cooking time – 20- 30 min.*

Seafood Chowder

BORSCHT, POLISH or RUSSIAN BEET SOUP

4 raw beets	Shredded white
5 cups brown	leek, cabbage,
stock	beet, celery
1 onion stuck	to make 1¼ cups
with 1 clove	in all
Bunch of herbs	
A few caraway	Salt and pepper
seeds	Grated nutmeg
2 tbs. bacon	5 oz. sour
fat	cream *or*
	yogurt

Slice 3 beets and simmer them in the stock with the onion, clove, herbs, and caraway seeds for about 1 hr. or until the color has run into the soup and the flavor is no longer raw. Melt the fat and in it cook the shreds of vegetable and the finely grated 4th beet very gently for 10-15 min. Strain the stock and press the juice out of the beets into it. Add the shreds of vegetable and finish cooking them in the soup. Season; add a trace of nutmeg to the soup. Beat the sour cream or yogurt into the hot soup but do not allow it to boil; *or* put a spoonful of yogurt or sour cream into each soup plate before pouring in the soup.

6 servings   Cooking time – 1½ hr.

SEAFOOD CHOWDER

1 smoked haddock	3-4 tbs. cream
(1-1¼ lb.)	Salt and pepper
1-2 sliced onions	1¼ cups shelled
¾ cup diced raw	shrimps
potatoes	1½ cups peas,
2-3 skinned	canned *or* frozen
tomatoes	and cooked
2-3 tbs. butter *or*	2 tsp. freshly
margarine	chopped
1 tbs. flour	parsley

Cover the well-washed haddock with cold water, bring slowly to a boil, then remove and wash again. Skim off scum from the stock. Cook onions in a little of the stock until almost soft. Add potatoes and cook until soft. Cut tomatoes into eighths, discard seeds; simmer in remaining stock. Add tomatoes to other vegetables and cook a little. Meanwhile, free the haddock

flesh of skin and bones. Melt the fat, add flour, and cook for a few min. without browning. Remove from heat. Slowly stir the strained remaining stock into this roux. Cook gently for a few min., while stirring. Stir in the cream and season to taste. Add the vegetable mixture, then the haddock and shrimps, reserving a few. Add the drained peas. Heat through, but do not boil. Sprinkle in the parsley, turn into a serving dish, and garnish with the reserved shrimps.

4 - 5 servings

FRIED SMELT

Smelt	Cayenne *or*
Ice	black pepper
Flour	Salt
Deep fat for	Lemon
frying	

Frying smelt is a difficult task for inexperienced cooks. The following is a well-tried method that, if carefully followed, usually produces satisfactory results. Put the smelt with a piece of ice in a bowl, which must be kept cool. When required for cooking, spread the fish on a cloth to dry, dredge well with flour, place in a wire basket, and shake off the superfluous flour. Plunge the basket into a pan of clean, very hot lard and fry rapidly for 3-4 min. Move the basket constantly while frying. Lift the basket, shake it to strain off the fat, and turn the dish onto waxed paper. Place on a warm dish and repeat until all the smelt are fried. Season with cayenne or black pepper and fine salt. Serve garnished with quarters of lemon.

COQUILLES OF COOKED HALIBUT or TURBOT

1¼ cups white	Browned
sauce	bread crumbs
¾ lb. cooked	Salt and pepper
halibut *or* turbot	Butter
Grated cheese	

Flavor the sauce with grated cheese to taste. Divide the fish into large flakes, put into 6 buttered scallop shells, cover with sauce, and sprinkle thickly with browned bread crumbs. Season, put 1 or 2 small pieces of butter on each, and cook for 15-20 min. in a moderate oven (180 °C, 350 °F).

6 servings

MUSSELS — CHOOSING AND PREPARING

Mussels are bought while still alive, and their shells should be tightly shut. Discard any that do not shut immediately when given a sharp tap, as they are probably dead. Mussels are in season from September to March. They can be served cold with vinegar or hot in soups, sauces, or pies. To prepare mussels, allow 2½-3¾ cups mussels per person. Scrape and clean the shells thoroughly in several lots of cold water. Mussels are not opened with a knife like oysters, but open themselves during cooking. The only part of a mussel that needs to be removed is the breathing apparatus which is found in the form of a black strip known as the "beard." This is removed after the shells have been opened.

There are two simple methods of opening mussels:

English method

For a small quantity of 2½-5 cups, place the mussels (after cleaning) in a rinsed wide pan and cover them. Heat quickly, shaking the pan at intervals, and after 5-7 min. the shells will open. Remove from the heat promptly; overcooking toughens them.

French method

To 8¾ cups of cleaned mussels in a wide pan, add 1 shallot, finely chopped, 5-6 stalks of parsley, a sprig of thyme, ⅓ of a bay leaf, a pinch of pepper, and ⅝ cup dry white wine (½ water and ½ dry cider can be used). Cover the pan tightly and cook over high heat for 5-6 min., shaking the pan from time to time. Remove from the heat as soon as the shells open.

MUSSELS FLORENTINE

12 fresh or canned mussels	1¼ cups milk
	Seasoning
12 oz. spinach	A little grated cheese
3 tbs. butter	
4 tbs. flour	

Cook the spinach. Put the shellfish in a small saucepan and add their liquor, previously strained through muslin. Poach for 2-3 min., until the edges just begin to ruffle slightly, then remove from the heat. Melt the butter in a saucepan, stir in the flour, and cook for 2 min. Add the milk, stir until boiling, and boil for 3 min. Cool slightly, then add the shellfish and their liquor. Drain the spinach and spread over the bottom of a casserole dish, pour the sauce on top, sprinkle with finely grated cheese, and brown lightly under a broiler. Serve immediately.

2- 3 servings

MOULES MARINIÈRES

8¾ cups mussels	Pinch of pepper
1 shallot, chopped finely	⅝ cup dry white wine (½ water and ½ dry cider can be used)
5-6 stalks of parsley	
⅓ of a bay leaf	2 tbs. butter
Sprig of thyme	Chopped parsley

Open the mussels by the French method. Strain the liquid through muslin to remove any traces of sand, then return the liquid to the pan with the butter and boil rapidly until reduced by half. Meanwhile, remove the beards from mussels, and return the mussels to their half shells; discard empty shells. Arrange in soup plates, pour the reduced liquor over the mussels, and sprinkle with chopped parsley.

TROUT MEUNIÈRE

4 large *or* 8 small trout	⅜ cup butter
	1 level tsp. chopped parsley
1 tbs. lemon juice	
Lemon "butterflies"	
A little seasoned flour	

Mussels Florentine

Lamb Kebabs

Dredge the trout lightly but thoroughly with seasoned flour. Heat the butter in a frying pan and, when hot, fry the trout until golden brown and cooked through. Arrange the trout on a hot dish. Reheat the fat until it is nut-brown in color; then pour it over the fish. Sprinkle the lemon juice and parsley over the fish, garnish with lemon "butterflies," and serve at once.

4 servings

FILETS OF SOLE WITH CREAM SAUCE

1 large sole	2½ cups milk *or*
Salt and pepper	milk and fish
Lemon juice	stock
1 small piece	¼ cup butter
of onion	⅜ cup flour
¼ tsp. ground	Parsley to
mace	garnish
	2 tbs. cream

Wash, skin, and filet the sole, and divide each filet lengthwise into two. Tie each strip loosely in a knot, or fold the ends over each other. Place in a greased pan, season with salt and pepper, sprinkle with lemon juice, cover with aluminum foil,

and bake for 10-15 min. in a moderate oven (180 °C, 350 °F). Simmer the bones of the fish, the onion and mace in the milk for about 15 min., then strain and season to taste. Melt the butter in a saucepan, add the flour, cook for 3-4 min., then pour in the flavored milk and stir until boiling. Let the sauce simmer for at least 10 min., then add cream; arrange the fish filets on a hot dish, either in a circle or forming 2 rows, and strain the sauce over. Decorate with a little chopped parsley.

4 servings

SOLE A LA PORTUGAISE

1 medium	1 onion
sole	2-3 tomatoes
2 tbs. butter	2 tsp. grated
1 shallot	Parmesan
1 tsp. finely	cheese
chopped parsley	2 tsp. browned
½ tsp. anchovy	bread crumbs
liquor	Extra butter
Salt and pepper	

Skin the sole and make an incision down the center as for fileting; raise the flesh from the bone on each side as far as possi-

Lamb Cutlets en Papillotes

ble. Mix the butter, finely chopped shallot, parsley, and anchovy liquor together well, and stuff the mixture inside the sole. Place the fish in a buttered casserole dish; season. Arrange slices of onion and tomato alternately and overlapping each other on top of the fish; if less onion is preferred, surround each slice of tomato with a single ring of onion. Mix together the cheese and bread crumbs and sprinkle over the fish. Place small pieces of butter on top, cover with lid, and bake for about 20 min. in a moderate oven (180 °C, 350 °F).

Filets of sole can be laid on a bed of the stuffing and cooked in the same way. Omit the onion and tomato rings if desired.

2 servings

19

SALMON CUTLETS MORNAY

2 slices of salmon, ¾-1 in. thick	Salt and pepper
	¼ cup flour
	⅝ cup cream
1 onion	1 tbs. grated Parmesan cheese
5 tbs. butter	
1¼ cups fish stock	
Bouquet Garni	2 tsp. lemon juice

Chop the onion coarsely. Melt half the butter in a shallow saucepan, fry the onion and salmon quickly on both sides, then add the stock (boiling), the Bouquet Garni, salt, and pepper. Cover and simmer gently for 20 min. Meanwhile, melt the remainder of the butter in another saucepan, add the flour, and cook 4 min. When the dish is done, transfer it to a hot dish and keep it warm. Strain the stock onto the flour and butter and stir until boiling. Simmer for 5 min., then add the cream, cheese, lemon juice, and seasoning to taste. Pour the mixture over the fish and serve.

DRESSED LOBSTER

Prepare the boiled lobster. Leave the meat in the shell and arrange the 2 halves on a bed of salad. Garnish with the claws. Serve with oil and vinegar passed separately. Piped Lobster Butter may be used to garnish the shell, if wished.

LOBSTER MAYONNAISE

1 boiled lobster	Salad
Mayonnaise	

Lobster Mayonnaise may be served in any of the following ways:

1) Serve like dressed lobster but with mayonnaise instead of oil and vinegar.

2) Cut the lobster in half lengthwise, scoop out the meat from the body, mix with a little mayonnaise, and return. Carefully remove the meat from the tail, slice and return to the shell, arranging it in overlapping slices with the red part uppermost. Serve on a bed of salad, garnished with the claws. Serve mayonnaise separately.

3) Remove all the meat from the shell and claws. Arrange on a bed of salad, either cut into slices or roughly flaked, and coat with mayonnaise.

The coral can be used, sieved, as a garnish.

BEEF STROGANOFF

2 lb. filet of beef	¼ cup butter
	A little brown stock
Flour	
Salt and pepper	1¼ cups sour cream
1 large onion	
2 cups chopped mushrooms	

Cut the beef into small, very thin pieces and shake in a wire sieve with a mixture of flour, salt, and pepper. Chop the onion. Heat the butter in a saucepan and fry the onion until golden brown. Add the beef and chopped mushrooms, fry a little, then moisten with the stock. Stir, and continue cooking for about 15-20 min. Add the sour cream, reheat, and serve.

6 servings   Time – 40 min.

BEEF A LA MODE

2 lb. rump of beef	2 tbs. butter *or* fat
½ cup claret	10 button onions
Juice of ½ lemon	¼ cup flour
1 small onion	3¾ cups stock
2 cloves	2 bacon slices
Salt and pepper	2 carrots
Bouquet Garni	

Trim and bone the meat. Place it in a bowl with a marinade made from the claret, lemon juice, finely chopped onion, cloves, salt, pepper, and Bouquet Garni. Leave for 2 hr., basting frequently. Melt the fat in a stewpan, drain the beef well, and fry until brown. Fry the button onions at the same time. Remove both from the pan, add the flour, and fry until nut-brown. Then add the stock and the marinade in which the meat was soaked and stir until boiling. Replace the meat and onions; season to taste. Cover the meat with the bacon slices. Add the carrots, thinly sliced, and cook gently for 2½ hr., stirring occasionally. When tender, place on a hot dish, strain the liquid in the saucepan, and pour over the meat.

8 servings

TOURNEDOS OF BEEF A LA NELSON

1½-2 lb. filet of beef, cut as tournedos	½ cup Madeira (optional)
1 cup small button onions	1¼ cups brown or Espagnole Sauce
Stock	1 cup diced potatoes
Salt and pepper	

Ask the butcher to prepare the tournedos. Parboil the onions in strong stock and then strain them. Fry the tournedos very lightly in hot fat to seal them; drain, and place in individual casseroles. Season with salt and pepper and add the onions. Add the wine to the sauce, season to taste, and add to the casseroles. Cook in a moderate oven (180 °C, 350 °F) for about 40 min. Fry the potatoes in hot fat until well-browned. Drain well and add to the casseroles 10 min. before serving.

6 servings

LAMB CUTLETS EN PAPILLOTES

6 lamb cutlets	2 tsp. chopped parsley
A few slices cooked ham	Salt and pepper
Salad oil or butter	Grated rind of ½ lemon
1 onion	
2 tsp. chopped mushrooms	

Prepare and trim the cutlets neatly. Cut 12 small rounds of ham just large enough to cover the round part of the cutlet. Melt a little fat in a pan and fry the finely chopped onion until tender. Add the mushroom, parsley, salt, pepper, and a little grated lemon rind. Mix well and then cool. Prepare 6 heart-shaped pieces of strong white paper large enough to hold the cutlets. Grease them well with oil or butter. Place a slice of ham on one half of each paper with a little of the chopped mixture on top. Lay the cutlet on the mixture, with more of the mixture on top, and place a round of ham over that. Fold over the paper and twist the edges well together. Lay the prepared cutlets in a greased baking pan and cook for 30 min. in a fairly hot oven (190 °C, 375 °F). Serve in the papers on a hot dish. A little good sauce may be served separately.

This method of cooking can be used with a number of different stuffings. Fried bread crumbs mixed with chopped sautéed onions is good; so is a mixture of fresh white bread crumbs, capers, and a little garlic salt.

6 servings   Cooking time – about 30 min.

LAMB KEBABS

6 pieces of lamb, cut from leg	6 small mushrooms
3 small sliced onions	6 small tomatoes
6 thick bacon slices	Oil or melted butter
	12 bay leaves

Trim the meat into neat even-shaped cubes. Cut the bacon in squares, and slice the tomatoes. Brush all (including tomatoes) with oil or butter and thread onto 6 skewers, interleaving with bay leaves. Grill for 10-15 min., turning as required. Serve on their skewers and, if liked, on a bed of risotto (rice cooked in stock in a casserole until stock is absorbed).

6 servings

WIENER SCHNITZEL

6 filets of veal about ½ in. thick	2½ cups dry bread crumbs
Salt and pepper	⅜ cup butter
1 tbs. flour	1 lemon
1 egg	

See that each filet is neatly trimmed, lay them on a board, and beat with a meat mallet. Sprinkle the filets with salt and pepper. Put the flour on a plate, and lightly coat each filet. Beat the egg and dip each filet into it. Coat the filets with bread crumbs. Put the butter into a frying pan and, when it is hot, fry the filets on each side to a rich golden brown. Drain and garnish with lemon.

6 servings

21

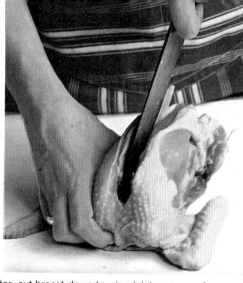

CUTTING BIRDS
Top, cut legs from body, cut wing tips off.

Center, cut breast down to wing joint, remove wing.

Bottom, split back .

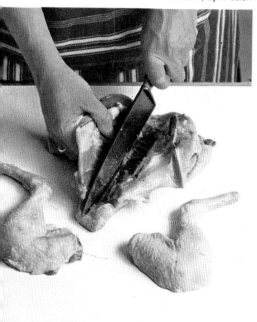

BRAISED PORK CHOPS IN CIDER

4 pork chops	Salt and pepper
4 tbs. cider	2-3 large
Bouquet Garni	mushrooms
3 onions	2 cups *or* 10-oz.
2 cooking apples	can garden peas
Good pinch of	2 cups *or* 10-oz.
ground	can beets
cinnamon	3 cups noodles

Trim off rind and excess fat and quickly fry chops in them until golden brown. Place in a casserole, add cider and Bouquet Garni, cover, and cook gently on the range or in a cool oven (150-170 °C, 300-325 °F). Meanwhile, pour off excess fat from frying pan; peel, chop, then fry the onions and apples for a few minutes. Add the cinnamon and water to cover them, put on a lid, and simmer until soft. Strain, season to taste, and add to the chops. Cover and cook for 1¾-2 hr. in all, adding the thickly sliced mushrooms ½ hr. before the end. Heat the peas and beets separately. Pour the noodles into salted boiling water and boil until, on testing a piece, the center is still slightly firm (about 8 min.). Drain the noodles, peas, and beets. Serve the noodles with the chops on top and garnish with the mushrooms, peas, and beets.

4 servings

Chicken with Supreme Sauce

BOILED HAM WITH OLIVES

Ham roast	Black olives
Apricot jam or syrup	Chopped parsley
	Piquant Sauce

Soak the ham for at least 2 hr., changing the water at the end of 1 hr. if very salty. Scrape the underside and rind as clean as possible. Put into a pan with cold water to cover. Bring to simmering point, remove any scum, then simmer for 20-25 min. per lb. until tender. When done, remove from the water, strip off the skin, and drain well. Spread with apricot jam, honey, or molasses, and put in a very hot oven (400 °F) for a few moments to glaze. Then sprinkle with chopped, stoned black olives and chopped parsley. Serve with Piquant Sauce and with Boiled Potatoes or Pea Pudding.

KIDNEYS WITH ITALIAN SAUCE

1½ lb. calves' kidneys	6-8 small onions
½ cup seasoned flour	2½ cups Italian Sauce
¼ cups beef drippings	Long-grained boiled rice
	Parsley

23

Prepare the kidney by cutting into ½-in. slices after removing skin and core. Coat the kidney well with seasoned flour. Heat the drippings in a sauté pan and fry the kidney quickly on both sides, then slowly for 10 min. with a lid on the pan. Sauté the onions at the same time, and shake the pan occasionally to turn them. Drain the kidney from the fat, place in the sauce, and simmer for about ¾ hr. Serve hot, garnished with long-grain boiled rice and parsley.

6 servings

ROAST CHICKEN, FRENCH STYLE

1 roasting chicken	Salt and pepper
2 tbs. butter	1 cup chicken
1 small onion	stock
1 carrot	
2 *or* 3 slices	
of bacon	

Garnish:

Watercress

Truss the chicken for roasting, and spread the breast thickly with butter. Slice the vegetables, place them in a roasting pan with bacon and the washed liver and heart of the bird; fry gently. Place the bird on the mirepoix of vegetables. Roast in a hot oven (220 °C, 425 °F) for 1-1½ hr., until tender. Cover the breast with a lid if it browns too quickly; baste if necessary. When cooked, remove trussing string. Keep the chicken hot. Drain the fat from the roasting pan, add stock, boil 2-3 min., season, and strain into gravy boat. Serve with gravy, and garnish with watercress.

Instead of gravy, the chicken can be served with 1 pt. Italian Sauce, white or brown, and with diced carrot, turnip, leek and celery, cooked for food value.

5- 6 servings

COQ AU VIN

1 3-lb. roasting	2 tbs. brandy
chicken *or*	1 carrot
chicken parts	1 onion
Stock	1 clove garlic

¼ lb. pickled	Bouquet Garni
belly of pork	(2 if possible)
or green bacon	Salt and pepper
6-8 oz. button	3 small fried
mushrooms,	croutes per
fresh *or* canned	person, round
2 tsp. tomato	*or* triangular,
puree (optional)	12 in all
3¾ cups red	Beurre Manié
wine	
12-16 pickling	
onions	

Cut up the chicken, if whole. Make a little stock from the giblets or a chicken stock cube, if necessary. Cut the pork into small cubes with extra fat if needed and fry slightly. Add the chicken pieces and fry until golden. Add the mushrooms and tomato puree, if used, and the onions. Toss in the fat. Heat the brandy, light it, and pour it over the chicken. Shake the pan until the flames die down. Add the stock and wine, carrot, onion, garlic, Bouquet, and seasoning. Cover the pan and simmer for 40 min. or until the chicken pieces are tender. Remove the chicken and vegetables, etc., discard the carrot, onion, and Bouquet, and keep the rest hot in the oven, with the fried croutes. Strain the wine sauce into a clean sauce-pan. Add the Beurre Manié in small pieces and stir until dissolved in the sauce. Simmer until the sauce is reduced to the consistency you want, but do not boil. Lay the croutes in a hot casserole, with the chicken on top, pour the sauce over, and serve very hot.

CHICKEN WITH SUPREME SAUCE

1 chicken	3¾ cups white
¾ cup Supreme	stock (approx.)
Sauce	

Garnish:

Macédoine of vegetables *or* **grape garnish as below**

Truss the chicken, poach it in the stock until tender, then divide into neat pieces. Arrange the pieces on a hot dish, pour the sauce over, and garnish with the chopped macédoine of vegetable piled at either end of the dish.

As an alternative garnish, toss 1 chopped red pepper and 1 cooked potato (sliced) in the sauce before pouring it over the chicken. Top with black and green grapes.

4 - 6 servings   Cooking time – about 1½- 2 hr.

CURRIED CHICKEN DUCHESSE

1 boiled chicken *or* 1-lb. can of chicken	5 tbs. cream *or* milk
2½ cups curry sauce	1 egg
	Salt and pepper
	Juice of 1 lemon

Garnish:

Chopped parsley
Croutons of fried bread *or* Creamed potato border

Cut the chicken into parts; remove skin and excess fat. Make sauce, thoroughly heat chicken in it, add cream and egg, stir over a low heat until the sauce thickens, but do not boil. Season; add lemon juice. Arrange chicken in an entree dish, strain sauce over, and garnish.

If a potato border is used, fork this into the dish before arranging the chicken for serving.

6 servings   Cooking – time 20 min. (excluding sauce)

CURRY SAUCE, MILD

1 medium onion	1¼ cups pale stock, coconut infusion (*see* below), *or* water
2 tbs. butter *or* margarine	
1 small cooking apple	½ tsp. molasses
1-2 tsp. curry powder	1-2 tsp. lemon juice
2 tbs. rice flour *or* flour	2 tsp. chutney
	Salt

Chop the onion, put it into a saucepan, and fry it very gently in the butter for 10 min. Chop the apple and cook it in the

butter with the onion for another 10 min. Stir in the curry powder and heat it for a few min. Add the flour and then stir in the liquid. When boiling, add all the other ingredients and simmer the sauce for at least ½ hr., or, better, 1½ hr.

To make the coconut infusion Soak ⅓ cup desiccated *or* fresh grated coconut in 1¼ cups water for a few minutes, bring slowly to boiling point, and steep it for 10 min. Wring the coconut in a piece of muslin to extract all the liquid.

STUFFED DUCKLING

1 large 4-5 lb. duckling	Sections of 1 large orange *or* apple and sauerkraut dressing
Fat for basting	
¾ cups brown sauce	

Stuffing:

1 chicken liver	Salt and pepper
1 duckling liver	Nutmeg
½ tsp. parsley	2 tbs. butter
¼ tsp. thyme	1 egg
2 cups bread crumbs	

Blanch chicken and duckling livers, chop them finely, add herbs, bread crumbs, melted butter, pinch of nutmeg, salt, and pepper. Bind this stuffing with egg. Stuff the duckling; truss, baste well with hot fat, and roast in a hot oven (220-230 °C, 425-450 °F) for ½ hr., basting frequently. Drain off all the fat, pour the hot brown sauce into the baking pan, and continue cooking until the duckling is tender (about 20 min.). Baste frequently with sauce. Serve on a hot dish. Strain a little sauce around, garnish with orange sections (heated in a little wine or stock, over a pan of hot water), and serve the remainder of the sauce separately.

Serve a dressing of canned sauerkraut with cored apple slices tossed in butter instead of the orange, if you wish.

4 servings   Cooking time – 1 hr.

Curried Chicken Duchesse

LIMA BEANS WITH CREAM SAUCE

2 lb. lima beans	1 lump of sugar
A bunch of herbs (thyme, sage, savory, marjoram, parsley stalks, or any one of these)	1 egg yolk
	⅝ cup light cream or evaporated milk
1¼ cups veal or chicken stock	Salt and pepper

Shell the beans and cook them in the stock with the lump of sugar and the bunch of herbs. When the beans are tender, lift out the herbs. Beat the egg yolk with the cream and stir it carefully into the saucepan. Reheat, stirring all the time, until almost simmering. Season, and serve at once.

TWO WAYS WITH FRENCH BEANS

1½ lb. French beans	Salt
2 tbs. butter or margarine	

Wash, top, tail, and string the beans. Do not cut up French beans, as they lose their flavor in cooking. Have ready just enough boiling salted water to cover them, and cook them with the lid on the pan. When tender (15-20 min.), drain and reheat in butter or margarine. Serve immediately.

For the French method of cooking, drain the cooked beans well, and shake in the pan until most of the water has evaporated. Add a little butter, parsley, lemon juice, and seasoning and shake over heat for a few minutes. Serve immediately.

4- 6 servings

COOKED MIXED VEGETABLES

1½ lb. mixed vegetables:

In winter: **parsnips, turnips, carrots, leeks, cauliflower**

In summer: **new carrots, new turnips, lima beans, peas, spring onions, tomatoes**

2 tbs. butter *or* margarine	Salt and pepper
¼-½ cup boiling water	Chopped parsley

Prepare all the vegetables. Cut the winter vegetables into thin slices, cutting large slices in halves or quarters. Break the cauliflower into flowerets. Leave most of the summer vegetables whole, cutting the carrots in thick slices, if not really small; trim the spring onions rather short; cut the tomatoes into wedges. Melt the fat in a saucepan. Add the vegetables to it at intervals, starting with those that take longest to cook. Put the lid on the pan after each addition and toss the vegetables in the fat. (Do not add the tomatoes to the summer vegetables until 5 min. before serving.) Add the liquid and the salt (use very little water with the summer vegetables), and simmer gently until the vegetables are tender. Serve hot, sprinkled with chopped parsley.

6 servings   Cooking time – winter vegetables, about ¾ hr.; summer vegetables, about ½ hr.

RED CABBAGE WITH APPLES

1 small red cabbage	1 tbs. corn syrup
2 tbs. margarine	Juice of ½ lemon
1 onion, chopped very fine	2 tbs. vinegar
2 cooking apples	Salt

Melt the fat. Add the onion and fry gently until light brown. Add finely shredded cabbage, peeled and sliced apples, and syrup. Cook over very gentle heat for 10 min., shaking pan frequently. Add lemon juice, vinegar, and salt and simmer, covered, 1-1½ hr. Stir occasionally. Season and serve.

6 servings

Braised Celery

BROCCOLI

This vegetable is known to the cook in three different forms:

1) Most cauliflowers sold between October and June come from the broccoli plant, which is very hardy. (The cauliflower plant proper is less hardy and supplies the typical white heads during the summer and early fall, before the frosts.) This form of broccoli is cooked by the methods suggested for cauliflower.

2) The Calabresse, green or Italian sprouting broccoli, produces a medium-sized green central head and is usually available in March. It is cooked like cauliflower and served with melted butter. After the central head is cut, shoots appear from every leaf joint, each shoot having a tiny head. The shoots are cut with about 6 in. of stem and provide an excellent vegetable for 2 or 3 months. The stems should be cut into short lengths and cooked, with the tiny heads, in boiling salted water as for any green vegetable; or they can be tied in bundles and cooked and served like asparagus.

3) Early purple-sprouting and white-sprouting broccoli come into season at the beginning of April. The tiny heads should be cut off with about 2 in. of stem and adjoining leaves and cooked whole in boiling salt water like any other green vegetable. The more the heads are cut off, the more prolific is the growth.

Frozen broccoli is available most of the

year. It should be cooked in very little water until just tender, and served with melted butter and a sprinkling of ground nutmeg or thyme.

BRAISED CELERY

| 4 heads of celery | Glaze |
| Stock | (if available) |

Mirepoix:

1 tbs. drippings	Watercress to
1/2 oz. bacon	garnish
2 large carrots	1 bay leaf
1 small turnip	Salt
2 onions	
Bouquet Garni	
(thyme,	
marjoram, sage,	
parsley)	

Trim the celery, but leave the heads whole. Wash them well and tie each securely. Prepare the mirepoix. Fry the bacon in the drippings in a large saucepan, then fry all the vegetables cut in pieces 3/4 in. thick, until lightly browned. Add herbs, spices, 1/2 tsp. of salt, and enough stock to come 3/4 of the way up the vegetables. Bring to boiling point. Lay the celery on top. Baste well with the stock in the pan and cover with a lid or aluminum foil. Cook until the celery is soft (about 1 1/2 hr.). Baste several times during cooking. Dish the celery and keep it hot. Strain the liquor, put it back in the pan, and add 1 tsp. of glaze, if available. Reduce by boiling quickly until of glazing consistency. Pour over the celery.

Note: Use the coarse outer stems of the celery for soups. A few pieces may be cut up and fried for the mirepoix. The cooked mircpoix can be served sprinkled with parsley as a separate vegetable dish or, if strained and thinned down with stock, it makes an excellent soup.

4 - 8 servings, according to the size of the celery heads

BOILED, MASHED, OR CREAMED POTATOES

2 lb. even-sized	Salt
potatoes,	Chopped parsley
old or new	

Scrub the potatoes. Peel or scrape thinly, if desired. Rinse and put into a saucepan with enough boiling water to cover, and 1 tsp. salt per qt. water. Boil gently for 15-40 min., according to age and size. Test with a fine skewer. When cooked, drain, steam-dry for a moment over low heat, and serve hot, sprinkled with chopped parsley.

For Mashed Potatoes, use:

2 lb. potatoes	A little milk
2 tbs. butter or	Salt and pepper
margarine	Grated nutmeg
Chopped parsley	

Prepare and cook peeled potatoes as for Boiled Potatoes, pass them through a sieve or a potato masher, or mash with a fork. Melt the fat (in one corner of the pan if the potatoes have been mashed in the pan itself) and beat in the potatoes. Add milk gradually and beat well until the mixture is thoroughly hot and smooth. Season well and add a little grated nutmeg. Serve in a hot dish. Sprinkle with chopped parsley.

Successful Mashed Potatoes depend on the use of a floury type of potato, thorough drying of the potatoes after the water has been strained off them, and thorough mashing of the potatoes before the fat and milk are added.

For Creamed Potatoes, add 1 tbs. cream (light or heavy) to Mashed Potatoes.

CHOCOLATE CHOUX OR PROFITEROLES

4 oz. Chou Pastry as below
Confectioners' sugar

Filling:

Sweetened whipped cream
5/8 cup Chocolate Sauce

Chou Pastry:

1 cup flour	1/2 tsp. vanilla
1 1/4 cups water	extract
1/2 tsp. salt	1 egg yolk
1/4 cup butter or	2 eggs
margarine	

Sift and warm the flour. Place water, salt,

and fat in a pan, and bring to boiling point. Remove from heat, add flour at once, and beat well over the heat again, until it becomes a smooth, soft paste and leaves the sides of the pan clean. Remove from the heat, add vanilla and egg yolk immediately, and beat well. Add the other 2 eggs 1 at a time, beating thoroughly between each addition. (It is important to get the first of the egg in while the mixture is hot enough to cook it slightly, otherwise it becomes too soft.) Add any flavoring last. Use while tepid.

Put the pastry into a pastry bag and pipe balls onto a greased baking sheet, using a 1-in. pipe; or shape the mixture with a spoon into piles. Bake in a fairly hot oven (200-220 °C, 400-424 °F) for 30 min. (do not open the door), then reduce the heat to 170 °C, 325 °F, for about 10 min., until the buns are dried inside. Cover with aluminum foil if they are becoming too brown. Split the buns and remove any damp mixture. Dry in the turned-off oven for a few moments if very damp.

For baby cream buns or Choux, sometimes called Profiteroles, use a tsp. or small pastry bag to shape the pastry into walnut-sized piles. Bake for 10 to 12 min. at the higher heat, and a further 5-8 min. at the reduced heat. Split, and dry out like cream buns, if required. Do not under-bake.

When the Choux or Profiteroles are cold, fill with sweetened whipped cream mixed with 1 tbs. Chocolate Sauce. Replace the tops and dust with confectioners' sugar. Serve the rest of the sauce separately.

These baby Choux are attractive among a selection of Petits Fours.

CHOCOLATE SAUCE

4 rounded tsp. cocoa	2 rounded tsp. sugar
2 rounded tsp. cornstarch	1¼ cups water
1 tbs. butter	3 drops vanilla extract

Blend together the cornstarch, cocoa, and sugar with a little of the water. Boil remaining water and pour onto blended mixture. Return to pan and boil for 2 min., stirring constantly. Add vanilla and butter. Serve hot or cold.

CARAMEL CUSTARD

⅜ cup sugar	⅝ cup milk
5 tbs. cold water	A few drops of vanilla extract
4 eggs	
2 tbs. sugar	

Have ready a warm charlotte or plain mold.

Prepare caramel with sugar and water by heating together without stirring until golden brown. Pour into mold. Work the eggs and sugar together without beating them, and pour the warmed milk on them. Add the vanilla extract. Strain the custard into the mold, and cover with waxed paper. Steam very slowly for about ¾ hr., until the custard is set in the center; or stand the custard uncovered in a tray of warm water and bake in a warm oven (170 °C, 355 °F) until the center is set. This takes about 40 min. Turn the custard out carefully so that the caramel runs off and serves as a sauce.

Small Caramel Custards can be made in dariole molds. Cook for about 20 min.

6 servings

STRAWBERRY SHORTCAKE

2 cups plain flour	1½ tbs. ground almonds
⅛ tsp. salt	½ cup margarine
Pinch of baking powder	¼ cup sugar
	1 egg yolk

Filling:

1¼ pt. strawberries	⅝-1¼ cups whipped cream
Sugar to taste	

Sift flour, salt, and baking powder and mix with the ground almonds. Cream the fat and sugar and add egg yolk. Work in the flour mixture as for a cake of shortbread. Divide into 3 pieces and roll into rounds a good ¼ in. thick. Bake in a moderate oven (180 °C, 350 °F) until golden brown, then allow to become cold. Crush strawberries slightly with sugar to taste and add a little whipped cream. Spread this onto the first round of shortcake, cover with the second round, and so on, finishing with a layer of straw-

Fruit Flan

Coffee Ice Cream

berries. Pipe whipped cream on top and around edges. Decorate as desired.

Cooking time – 30- 40 min.

Note: Self-rising flour may be used if liked, without the baking powder. Pears make a good addition to the strawberries. Slice the peeled pears, poach them, and drain well before using.

CHARTREUSE OF BANANAS
(A fancy full cream)

5 cups clear Lemon Jelly, as below	1¼ cups heavy cream
¼ cup pistachio nuts	Vanilla extract
4 bananas	Sugar to taste

Line a 1 qt. border or ring mold with jelly. Blanch, skin, chop, and dry the pistachio nuts; mix with 2 tbs. jelly and run smoothly over the base of the mold. When set, cover with a ½-in. layer of clear jelly. Slice a banana evenly, dip each slice in jelly, and arrange them, slightly overlapping, in an even layer on the jelly when set. Cover with another ½-in. layer of clear jelly and allow to set. Repeat with fruit and jelly until the mold is full, the last layer being jelly. When set, turn out and pipe the whipped cream, sweetened, and flavored with vanilla, into the center. Surround with chopped jelly.

Strawberries or tangerines may be substituted for bananas and the chartreuse named accordingly.

6 servings   Setting time – without ice: 2- 3 hr; with ice: ¾ hr.

30

Pear and Strawberry Shortcake

LEMON JELLY

4 lemons	1-in. cinnamon
Sherry (optional)	stick
3¾ cups water	⅓ cup gelatin
¾ cup sugar	Shells and whites
4 cloves	of 2 eggs

Scald a large pan, wire whisk, and metal jelly mold. Wash the lemons and cut thin strips of rind, omitting the white pith. Extract juice and measure. Make up to 1¼ cups with water *or* sherry, but do not add sherry until just before clearing the jelly. Put the water, juice, rinds, sugar, flavorings, and gelatin into the scalded pan and steep, with a lid on, over very gentle heat until sugar and gelatin are dissolved. Do not let the infusion become hot. Wash and crush egg shells. Lightly whisk the whites until liquid and add, with shells, to the infusion. Heat steadily, whisking constantly, until a good head of foam is produced and the contents of the pan become hot but not quite boiling. Strain through the crust as described above, and add the sherry, if used, as the jelly goes through the filter.

6 servings   Time 1- 1½ hr.

FRUIT FLAN

Rich Shortcrust Pastry or Pâté Sucrée, using 1 cup flour, etc.

Filling:

1 medium-sized can of fruit *or* ¾ **lb. fresh fruit, e.g. strawberries, pears, pineapple, cherries, apricots, peaches, etc.**

Coating Glaze:

⅝ cup syrup from canned fruit *or* fruit juice *or* water Sugar (if necessary)	1 tsp. arrowroot Lemon juice to taste

Decoration (optional):

Sweetened whipped cream

Line a 7-in. flan ring with the pastry. Prick the bottom of the flan, and bake it until lightly browned. Bake for about 30 min., first in a fairly hot oven (200 °C, 400 °F), reducing the heat to moderate as the pastry sets (180 °C, 350 °F). Leave in oven for 5 min. to dry the bottom. Allow to cool. If fresh fruit is used, stew gently until tender, if necessary. Drain the fruit. Place the sugar, if used, and liquid in a pan and boil for 10 min. Blend the arrowroot with some lemon juice and add it to the syrup, stirring constantly. Continue stirring, cook for 3 min., then cool slightly. Arrange the fruit attractively in the flan case and coat it with fruit syrup.

If liked, the flan may be decorated with piped sweetened whipped cream.

For a quick flan or tart shell, a packaged crumb crust or cake mixture can be used satisfactorily.

CRÉME BRÛLÉE

1¼ cups fresh milk	Confectioners' sugar
1¼ cups cream	Chopped,
5 eggs	blanched
¼ cup sugar	almonds
Vanilla extract *or* brandy	(optional)

Heat milk and cream until almost boiling. Beat eggs and sugar together to blend well. Pour on the hot milk and cream, stirring well. Add vanilla *or* brandy to taste. Strain into a 1-qt. fireproof china soufflé case. Bake very gently for approximately 1 hr. in a very cool oven. Use a water bath if oven is hotter than 130 °C, 265 °F. When set, allow to cool, and dredge the surface to a depth of ⅛ in. with confectioners'

sugar. Sprinkle chopped almonds over lightly if liked. Broil until sugar has been changed to caramel. Serve cold with whipped cream.

Note: This recipe may be varied by substituting 2½ cups cream or half and half for 1¼ cups fresh milk and 1¼ cups cream and using 8 egg yolks instead of 5 whole eggs. Proceed as above.

6 servings

SAVARIN

1 cup plain flour	1 egg
Pinch of salt	½ tbs. sugar
1 tbs. yeast	3 tbs. butter
2½ tbs. warm water	

Kirsch Sauce:

⅜ cup sugar	1-2 tbs. kirsch
⅝ cup water	Juice of ½ lemon

Decoration:

Apricot jam
Blanched almonds, browned

Sift the flour and salt into a bowl and allow to warm. Cream the yeast with the tepid water. Make a well in the center of the flour and pour in the yeast mixture. Sprinkle over the top with a little of the flour from the side of the bowl. Let stand for 10-15 min. in a warm place. Add the egg gradually, beating well to a smooth elastic dough, using a little more tepid water if necessary. Knead well. Put the dough back into the bowl and press down, sprinkle the sugar on the top, and put on the butter in small pieces. Cover with a damp cloth and leave in a warm place to double its size. Beat well again until all the sugar and butter are absorbed. Grease a border mold and fill it ⅓ of the way up with the mixture.

Let stand in a warm place until the mixture just reaches the top of the mold. Then bake in a fairly hot oven (200 °C, 400 °F) for about 20 min.

Make the sauce: boil the water and sugar steadily for about 10 min. Add the kirsch and lemon juice.

Turn the Savarin out onto a hot dish, prick with a needle or pin, and soak well in the sauce. Coat with hot sieved apricot jam and decorate with spikes of almonds, etc. Serve with the rest of the sauce poured around.

A Savarin can be served with a Rum Sauce. Use rum instead of kirsch. It can also be served, hot or cold, with stewed cherries and stiffly whipped sweetened cream in the center. In this case, make the syrup with cherry brandy. Stiffly whipped sweetened cream mixed with crushed macaroons is another classic filling.

4 servings

CUSTARDS FOR ICE CREAM

BASIC CUSTARD WITH EGGS

2½ cups milk	½ cup sugar
3 eggs	

Heat the milk. Beat together the eggs and sugar. Add the hot milk slowly, stirring continuously. Return to the pan and cook without boiling until custard coats the back of a wooden spoon. Strain, cover, and cool.

RICH CUSTARD

2½ cups milk	2 eggs
8 egg yolks	½ cup sugar

Heat the milk. Beat together eggs and sugar until thick and white; add the milk. Cook, without boiling, until it thickens. Strain, cover, and cool.

BASIC ICE CREAM (VANILLA)

1¼ cups cream	1 tsp. vanilla
1¼ cups cold vanilla pudding *or* custard	¼ cup sugar

Half-whip the cream. Add the custard, vanilla, and sugar. Chill and freeze.

CHOCOLATE ICE CREAM

4 oz. plain chocolate	⅝ cup cream
5 tbs. water	1-2 tsp. vanilla extract
1¼ cups custard *or* pudding	

Break chocolate in pieces; place in pan; add water. Dissolve over low heat. Add melted chocolate to the custard. Cool. Add the half-whipped cream and vanilla to taste. Chill and freeze.

6 - 8 servings

RASPBERRY OR STRAWBERRY ICE CREAM

1 small can raspberries or strawberries	⅝ cup Basic Custard with Eggs, cold
⅝ cup cream	¼ cup sugar

Drain the fruit and pass it through a nylon sieve. The fruit and juice together should make 1¼ cups. Mix with the custard. Half-whip the cream and blend the 2 mixtures gradually. Add the sugar and a little food coloring if you wish. Chill, then freeze.

COFFEE ICE CREAM

1¼ cups cream	2 tbs. liquid coffee
1¼ cups Basic Custard with Eggs	¼ cup sugar

Make like Basic Vanilla Ice Cream.

MOLDING ICES

If the mixture is to be molded, it should be removed from the freezer or refrigerator in a semi-solid condition, then packed into a dry mold, shaken well, and pressed down into the shape of the mold. The mold should have a tight-fitting lid. It should be wrapped in waxed paper and buried in broken ice and freezing salt for 1½-2 hr.

To unmold, remove the paper, wipe the mold carefully, dip it into cold water, and turn the ice onto a dish in the same way as a jelly.

The Wedding

A wedding breakfast may be a formal luncheon or dinner party, with the Wedding Cake as the *pièce de résistance*. In this case the hostess chooses light but memorable dishes for her menu, taking particular care that they suit the champagne and other light wines that are usually served.

Very often, however, the traditional wedding breakfast gives place to a buffet-style meal, the type depending on the time of day the wedding takes place. A morning wedding may be followed by cocktail-style snacks; an afternoon buffet may consist of teatime dainties, or may be cocktail fare later in the day. No matter what the style, however, the focus of the buffet is always "the cake," and all other food is supplementary to its white glory. It should be placed in the center of the buffet or on a separate table where the bride and groom can cut it easily, and from which it can be distributed on trays, ready and waiting beforehand.

As for a formal wedding breakfast, all other food should suit the champagne, which is usually the principal wine.

WEDDING CAKE

Note: These quantities are sufficient for a 3-tier cake.

3-3¼ lb. flour	2 lb. raisins
¼ tsp. salt	1-1½ lb. glacé
3 level tsp.	cherries
ground	1-1¼ lb. mixed
cinnamon	chopped candied
3 level tsp.	fruit peel
ground mace	Rind and juice
1 nutmeg (grated)	of 1 lemon
1½ tsp. baking	½-1 lb. blanched
powder	chopped
3 lb. butter	almonds
3 lb. sugar	1 cup rum *or*
1½ tsp. gravy	brandy *or* rum
brownings	and brandy
24 large eggs	
5½ lb. currants	

Prepare and line with greased paper 3 cake pans, one 12 in. diameter, one 8 in. and one 4 in. diameter. Sift together flour, salt, spices, and baking powder. Mix together all the fruit with a little of the measured flour. Cream the butter and sugar very well; add gravy brownings. Add egg and flour alternately to the creamed fat, beating well between each addition. Stir in the prepared fruit, almonds, and brandy. Divide ½ of the mixture between the 2 smaller pans, and put the remaining ½ of the

35

Three-Tier Wedding Cake

mixture in the biggest pan. Smooth the mixture and make a depression in the center of each cake. Bake the 4-in. cake for 2-3 hr., the 8-in. cake for 3½-4 hr., and the 12-in. cake for 5-6 hr. Put in a cool oven (150 °C, 310 °F) for the first ½ hr., then reduce heat to very cool (130-140 °C, 250-275 °F) for the remainder of the time.

To cover the 4-in. cake with Almond Paste, 1 lb. ground almonds, etc., will be required; 2 lb. ground almonds, etc., for the 8-in. cake; and 3 lb. ground almonds, etc., for the 12-in. cake.

For the Royal Icing use 1 lb. confectioners' sugar, etc., for the 4-in. cake; 2 lb. for the 8-in. cake; and 3 lb. sugar, etc., for the 12-in. cake.

Decoration of each cake is then completed on silver trays (of correct size) covered with a lace doily. The cake is then assembled by placing one cake on top of the other with pillars supporting them. The pillars for the bottom tier should be 3 in. height and for the top the pillars should be 4 in. high. Place a silver vase containing white flowers on top.

ALMOND PASTE (ICING)

Almond Paste — often called Almond Icing or Marzipan — is used to cover rich cakes before applying Royal or glacé icing. (It is also used alone to decorate cakes, e.g. Simnel Cake and Battenburg Cake.) It is often colored and flavored and then molded into various shapes to be used for cake decoration.

1½ cups confectioners' sugar and ¾ cup granulated sugar or 3 cups confectioners' sugar	¾ tsp. orange-flower water
	¾ tsp. vanilla extract
	1-2 egg yolks
2 cups ground almonds	
Juice of ½ lemon	

Sift the confectioners' sugar into a bowl and mix with the ground almonds and granulated sugar. Add the lemon juice, flower water, vanilla, and enough egg yolk to bind the ingredients into a pliable but dry paste. Knead thoroughly by hand until smooth.

Note: A whole egg or egg whites may be used instead of egg yolks. Egg yolk gives a richer and yellower paste, while egg white gives a whiter, more brittle paste. (Economically the yolks can be used for Almond Paste and the whites used for Royal Icing.) This quantity of paste is sufficient to cover the top and sides of an 8-in. cake.

To Apply Almond Paste

To cover the top and sides of a rich fruit cake, the cake top should be fairly level and the surface free from loose crumbs.

Brush the top and sides with warm Apricot Glaze, using a pastry brush. Dredge a little granulated sugar onto a clean board and roll out the Almond Paste to a round that is 4 in. wider than the diameter of the cake. Place the cake in the center of this with its glazed top downward and work the paste upward around the sides of the cake with the hands until it is within ¼ in. of the top edge, i.e. on the cake bottom. Using a straight-sided jar or thick tumbler, roll firmly around the sides, pressing slightly with the other hand on the up-turned bottom of the cake and turning the cake around on the sugared board when necessary.

Continue rolling and turning until the sides are straight and smoothly covered and the top edges of the cake are sharp and smooth, when the process is completed and the cake is turned upright.

Note: Allow a few days for the Almond Paste to dry before putting on the Royal Icing, or the oil from the Almond Paste will discolor it. Cover with a clean cloth to protect from dust while drying.

APRICOT GLAZE

2 tbs. apricot jam	1 tbs. water

Sieve the jam and water into a saucepan. Place over heat and bring to boiling point. Remove and cool. Use to glaze the tops of small cakes, to stick Almond Paste to Christmas Cakes, etc.

ROYAL ICING

1 lb. confectioners' sugar (approx.)	2 egg whites 1 tsp. lemon juice

If the sugar is lumpy, roll with a rolling pin before sifting. Put the egg whites into a bowl; beat slightly with a wooden spoon. Add 2 tsp. sifted sugar and beat again. Gradually add the remainder of the sugar, beating well until a thick, smooth consistency and a good white color are obtained. Add the lemon juice and beat again.

If a softer icing is required, 1 tsp. glycerine may be stirred in after the sugar; this prevents the icing becoming brittle and facilitates cutting.

If the icing is not wanted at once, cover the bowl with a damp cloth to keep it soft.

TO ICE A CAKE WITH ROYAL ICING

Place the cake, already covered with Almond Paste, on a cake board or inverted plate. Place the cake board on a turntable if available.

For an 8-in. cake, use:

First coating Royal Icing, using 1¼ lb. confectioners' sugar, etc., mixed to a stiff consistency.

Second coating ¾-1 lb. confectioners' sugar, etc., consistency to coat the back of a spoon.

Decorative piping ½ lb. confectioners' sugar, etc., mixed to a stiff consistency, i.e. that will stand up in points when the back of the spoon is drawn away from the side of the bowl.

To Apply First Coating

With a tbs. take enough icing to cover the top and place it in the center of the cake. Spread evenly over top, smoothing the surface with a hot, wet spatula (shake or dry the spatula after dipping it in hot water, as too much water softens the icing). Take up small portions of the icing with the end of the spatula; spread it smoothly around the side until the cake is completely covered and the surface smooth.

Allow to set for a few days before applying the second coat. While the icing is drying and as soon as it is hard enough, place a thin sheet of paper lightly over the top to protect it from dust.

To Apply Second Coating

Mix icing to a thin coating consistency and pour over the cake. Prick any bubbles with a fine skewer or pin; allow to firm before decorating.

Icing syringes are made of metal or plastic and can be bought in sets complete with decorative tubes. Excellent plastic turntables are also available. If colored icings are being used, the syringe must be washed before filling with another color. All tubes must be kept clean. Always keep the bowl containing the icing covered with a damp cloth while decorating, to prevent the icing drying out.

The beginner should practice on an upturned cake pan or plate before starting on the cake, and the icing may be removed if scraped off immediately and returned to the covered bowl.

For Christmas Cakes other decorations may be made with colored Marzipan, e.g. holly, Marzipan, apples, etc., and the smooth icing surface roughened into points with a spatula to form "snow drifts." For this, only one coat is needed.

Christmas and Other Traditional Festivities

Here are dishes that make a good Christmas dinner in truly traditional style. They are followed by menus that could be used by a small family or just two people. They are also suitable as Easter lunch or dinner menus.

All the recipes for these festivity menus are in this book. The section on *Dishes for Dinner Parties* especially will give the hostess ideas for other festivity meals.

After the menus, you will find recipes and suggestions for various cakes for special occasions.

TUNA SALAD IN GRAPEFRUIT

Allow 1 grapefruit for 2 helpings. Cut across in half and remove the pulp. Add to it an equal amount of drained canned peas and half this amount in flaked tuna fish moistened with mayonnaise. Cut out the core and skinny bits of the grapefruit and squeeze their juice into the grapefruit shells. Line the inside of the shells with shredded lettuce, heap the mixture into them, and sprinkle with paprika.

MELON

There are various kinds of melon. They must not be overripe, should be served as fresh as possible, and, above all, very cold.

Put crushed ice around the dish on which the slices of melon are served. Serve with powdered ginger and sugar.

TOMATO SOUP

1 lb. tomatoes,	Grated nutmeg
fresh *or* canned	Lemon juice
1 onion	A bunch of herbs
1 carrot	Minute tapioca
1 tbs. margarine	*or* cornstarch
1 oz. ham	Salt and pepper
scraps, rind,	Sugar
or bone	Red coloring,
2½ cups white	if needed
stock *or* juice	
from canned	
tomatoes	

Slice the tomatoes, onion, and carrot. If canned tomatoes are used, strain them and make the juice up to 2½ cups with stock. Melt the margarine in a deep pan and lightly fry the sliced vegetables and chopped ham for 10 min. Boil the stock or tomato juice and add to the vegetables with the nutmeg, lemon juice, and herbs and cook for ¾-1 hr. Sieve and thicken the soup with 2 tbs. cornstarch or minute tapioca to each 2½ cups of soup, blended with a little cold milk, stock, or water. Stir into the soup, cook until clear,

Roast Turkey

Tomato Soup

season, add sugar to taste, and coloring if needed.

    4 servings   Cooking time – ¾ - 1 hr.

ROAST TURKEY WITH APPLE AND RICE STUFFING

One 13-lb. turkey	Vienna *or* link
Apple and Rice	sausages
Stuffing	Bread Sauce *or*
2-3 slices	apple sauce
bacon	Stuffed Braised
Fat for basting	onions *or* apples
Gravy	

APPLE AND RICE STUFFING FOR TURKEY

1 chicken	1 lb. cooking
bouillon cube	apples,
1 cup long-	finely grated
grain rice	2 cups fresh

3 medium-sized onions, finely chopped	white bread crumbs
6 oz. frozen peas	1 egg to bind
Salt and pepper	Butter or margarine
4-5 oz. American cheese	

Dissolve the bouillon cube in 1½ cups water and bring to a boil. Add the rice and onions. Simmer gently for 10 min., until all the stock has been absorbed. Stir in the peas and allow the mixture to cool. Season carefully. Mix the cheese and grated apple together, and add carefully to the rice. Sprinkle on the bread crumbs, and stir in. Add the egg to bind the mixture. (This quantity is enough to stuff a 13-lb. turkey, leaving enough forcemeat mixture remaining to make 7 or 9 forcemeat balls.) Bake the forcemeat balls separately in foil, with butter or margarine to baste, for about 20 min. at 170 °C, 325 °F.

Stuff the crop of the bird, as well as the body, with Apple and Rice Stuffing. Truss the bird for roasting. Lay the bacon strips over the breast. Roast in a preheated hot oven (220 °C, 425 °F) for 15-20 min.; then reduce the heat to moderate (180 °C, 350 °F) and baste frequently until the bird is done. The cooking time will depend on the size and quality of the bird. As a general guide, allow 15 min. per lb. for a bird under 14 lb. in weight, 12 min. per lb. for one over 14 lb. About 20 min. before serving, remove the bacon to let the breast brown. Crumble it and add the crumbs to the sauce if wished.

When ready to serve, remove the trussing string. Serve with gravy, sausages, and Bread or Apple Sauce. Surround it with Stuffed Braised Onions or apples.

A young turkey or turkey pullet is cooked under aluminum foil instead of bacon strips and takes only about an hour in a hot oven (220 °C, 425 °F). It is usually served with thin gravy and fried bacon rolls or slices of hot boiled ham.

On a large turkey the breast meat may dry up in a small oven before the legs are cooked through. Either cover the breast with heavy-duty aluminum foil for the whole cooking time or remove the legs before cooking (or when the breast is ready) and cook them separately for another dish.

VARIATION

An attractive way of dealing with a frozen turkey is to season and baste it with fruit juice. In this case, it is best served with the Stuffed Braised Onions rather than the apples. For a 9-10 lb. frozen turkey, use:

1 orange	¼ tsp. dried rosemary
1 large onion	
1 dessert apple	¼ tsp. dried oregano
2 tbs. olive oil	
Salt and freshly ground black pepper	

Basting Juice:

½ cup melted butter	1 chicken bouillon cube
⅝ cup dry white wine	Salt and freshly ground black pepper
Juice of 2 oranges	
1 clove garlic, finely chopped	

STUFFED BRAISED ONIONS

6 large onions, peeled and parboiled	1 lb. cheddar cheese
1 lb. cooking apples, peeled, cored, and finely chopped	Salt and freshly ground black pepper
	¼ lb. frozen peas, thawed

Fully thaw the turkey before preparing any ingredients. Mix the orange segments, chopped onion and apple, olive oil, salt and pepper, and herbs. Season the inside of the bird with this mixture. Prepare the basting juice by mixing all the ingredients together. Roast the turkey in the usual way, but baste with the juice instead of with fat. While the turkey is cooking, parboil the onions, stuff them with the mixed apple, cheese, seasoning, and peas, and bake them in a shallow pan under the turkey until tender.

ROAST TURKEY WITH CHESTNUTS

1 turkey	Cream *or* milk
2-3 lb. chestnuts, dried *or* fresh	1-1½ lb. sausage meat *or* 1 lb.
1¼ cup chicken stock	Sausage Stuffing
¼ cup butter	2-3 slices bacon
1 egg	Fat for basting
Salt and pepper	Gravy
	Cranberry Sauce

If fresh, slit the chestnut skins, cook them in boiling water for 15 min., drain, and remove the skins. If dried, soak overnight, then simmer 15 min. in boiling water.

Stew the prepared chestnuts in stock for 1 hr.; drain, and then chop or sieve them, saving a few for garnish. Make the stuffing with the chopped chestnuts, butter (melted), egg, seasoning, and cream. Fill the crop of the bird with this stuffing and the body with sausage meat or stuffing, well-seasoned. Truss the bird for roasting. Cover it with bacon and roast in a moderate oven (180 °C, 350 °F) until tender, basting well. Times are given in the previous recipe. Toward the end of the cooking time, remove the bacon to let the breast brown. Remove the trussing string before serving. Garnish with the reserved chestnuts, and serve with gravy and Cranberry Sauce.

SAUSAGE STUFFING

½ lb. lean pork	Salt and pepper
1¼ cups bread crumbs	Grated nutmeg to taste
½ tsp. mixed fresh herbs *or* ¼ tsp. dried herbs	The liver of the bird to be stuffed
2 small sage leaves	Stock

Mince the pork. Chop the liver. Mix all the ingredients, using enough stock to bind the mixture. Season to taste. Use for turkey or chicken.

Note: A good bought pork-sausage meat mixed with the liver of the bird makes a quick stuffing for poultry.

BREAD SAUCE

1 large onion	1¼ cups milk
2 cloves	1¼ cups dry white bread crumbs
Pinch of ground mace	
1 bay leaf	1 tbs. butter
4 peppercorns	Salt and pepper
1 allspice berry	2 tbs. cream (optional)

Put the onion and spices into the milk; bring them very slowly to boiling point. Cover the pan and steep over a gentle heat for ½-1 hr. Strain the liquid. To it add the crumbs and butter, and season to taste. Keep the mixture just below simmering for 20 min. Stir in the cream if used; serve the sauce at once. Serve with roast chicken or turkey.

CRANBERRY SAUCE

2 cups cranberries	Sugar to taste
⅝-1¼ cups water	

Stew the cranberries until soft, using ⅝ cup water and adding more if needed. Rub the fruit through a hair or nylon sieve. Sweeten to taste. For economy, half cranberries and half sour cooking apples make an excellent sauce. Serve with roast turkey, chicken, or game.

GRAVY — for any roast except pork, and for poultry

Drippings from the roasting pan	Water in which vegetables have been boiled, *or* stock
Flour	
Juices from the roast *or* poultry	Salt and pepper

Drain most of the fat from the roasting pan, carefully saving any sediment and meat juices. Dredge into the thin film of drippings sufficient flour to absorb it all. Brown this flour slowly until a nut-brown color. Stir in water in which green vegetables or potatoes have been cooked, or stock, allowing 1¼ cups for 6 persons. Boil the gravy, and season it to taste.

Roast Goose and apples coated with cloves

To obtain a brown color without browning the flour, add a few drips of gravy brownings from the end of a skewer.

For giblet gravy for poultry, use chicken fat and stock made with giblets.

ROAST GOOSE

1 goose	Flour
Sage and Onion Stuffing	Apple Sauce
Fat for basting	Gravy (*see* below)

Prepare the goose, make the stuffing, and insert this in the body of the bird. Truss the goose, and prick the skin of the breast. Roast the bird in a fairly hot oven (190-200 °C, 375-400 °F) for 2½ hr. or until tender. When almost cooked, dredge the breast with flour, baste with some of the hot fat, and finish cooking. Remove trussing string. Serve with Apple Sauce and a gravy made with thickened beef stock. Goose giblet gravy is very rich.

8 - 10 servings

APPLES, APRICOTS, ETC., WITH MEAT

Apples are often baked whole and served with goose instead of apple sauce. They are cored but not peeled, and the core holes are stuffed with a little sage stuffing or with raisins, so that the apples keep their shape. They are cooked just like sweet baked apples.

SAGE AND ONION STUFFING

1 medium onion	1¼ cups bread crumbs
4 sage leaves *or* ½ tsp. powdered sage	2 tbs. butter
	Salt and pepper
	1 egg (optional)

Slice the onion thickly and parboil for 10 min. in very little water. Scald the sage leaves. Chop both. Mash all the ingredients together and season to taste.

APPLE SAUCE

3 medium apples	Rind and juice of ½ lemon
2 tbs. water	Sugar to taste
1 tbs. butter *or* margarine	

Stew the apples very gently with the water, butter, and lemon rind until they are pulpy. Beat them quite smooth or rub them through a hair or nylon sieve. Reheat

Brussels Sprouts with Chestnuts

Cauliflower with White Sauce

the sauce with the lemon juice and sweeten to taste.

For Apple Raisin Sauce, add ½ tbs. chopped parsley and 2 tbs. seedless raisins before reheating.

BOILED BRUSSELS SPROUTS WITH CHESTNUTS

1½ lb. brussels sprouts	12 cooked chestnuts
Salt	3 oz. chopped ham
2 tbs. butter or margarine (optional)	4 tbs. cream

Choose small, close sprouts. Remove shabby outer leaves by cutting the end, then make a cross cut on the bottom of each stalk. Soak in cold water containing 1 tsp. salt per qt., for 10 min. only. Wash thoroughly under running water if possible. Choose a suitably sized pan and put in enough water to ¼ fill it only, with ½ tsp. salt to 2½ cups of water. When boiling, put in half the sprouts, the largest if variable in size, put on lid, and bring quickly to boil again. Add rest of sprouts and cook until all are just tender, with the lid on the pan all the time. Drain in a colander and serve immediately in a hot vegetable dish or toss in melted butter before serving. Sprouts should be served quickly, as they soon cool.

To serve with chestnuts, put the sprouts, chopped chestnuts, ham, and cream into a casserole, cover and reheat in the oven at 180 °C, 350 °F.

6 servings   Cooking time – 15 min.

CHESTNUTS AU JUS

2 lb. chestnuts	Cayenne pepper
2 cloves	Salt
1 small onion	2 tsp. meat glaze (if available)
1 outside stalk of celery	
1 bay leaf	Fleurons of pastry
1 pinch of mace	
2½ cups brown stock	

Take a sharp knife and make an incision in each chestnut, in the shell only. Put into a saucepan and cover with cold water. Bring to a boil and cook for 2 min. Drain, peel, and skin the chestnuts while very hot. Stick the cloves into the onion and put chestnuts, onion, celery, bay leaf, and mace into the boiling stock. Season. Simmer about 1 hr., until the chestnuts are tender. Strain, and keep the chestnuts hot. Return stock to pan, add the meat glaze if available, and reduce to a glazing consistency. Pile the chestnuts in a hot vegetable dish, pour the glaze over, and decorate with fleurons of pastry.

For a puree, sieve the cooked chestnuts and add a little butter and cream to taste.

6 servings

43

CAULIFLOWER WITH WHITE SAUCE

1 large cauliflower	Salt
1¼ cups white sauce made with ½ milk and ½ cauliflower water	

Trim off the stem and all the leaves except the very young ones. Soak in cold water, head down, with 1 tsp. salt per qt. of water, for not more than 10 min. Wash well. Choose a suitably sized pan and put in enough water to ¼ fill it, with ½ tsp. salt to 2½ cups water. Put in cauliflower, stalk down, and cook with lid on pan until stalk and flower are tender. Lift out carefully and drain. Keep hot. Coat the cauliflower with the sauce and serve immediately.

Note: To reduce cooking time, the cauliflower may be quartered or broken into large flowerets before cooking.

6 servings   Cooking time – 20- 25 min.

GLAZED CARROTS

1½ lb. young carrots	¼ tsp. salt
¼ cup butter	Cook stock
3 lumps sugar	Chopped parsley

Melt the butter in a saucepan. Add the scraped whole carrots, sugar, salt, and enough stock to come halfway up the carrots. Cook gently, without a lid, shaking the pan occasionally until tender. Remove the carrots and keep them hot. Boil the stock rapidly until reduced to a rich glaze. Replace the carrots 2 or 3 at a time; turn them until both sides are well coated with glaze. Dish, sprinkle with chopped parsley, and serve.

6 servings   Cooking time – about ¾ hr.

GREEN PEAS

2 lb. peas	A little sugar
Salt	1 tbs. butter or margarine
Sprig of mint	

Shell the peas. Have sufficient boiling salted water to cover the peas. Add the peas, mint, and sugar. Simmer gently until soft, from 10-20 min. Drain well. Re-heat with butter or margarine and serve in a hot vegetable dish.

If the peas must be shelled some time before cooking, put them in a bowl and cover them with washed pea pods.

4- 6 servings (according to yield)

ROAST POTATOES

2 lb. even-sized potatoes	Salt and pepper Drippings

Peel the potatoes and cut in halves, or in quarters if very large. Parboil, strain off the water, and dry the potatoes over a low heat. Put into hot drippings in a roasting pan or in the pan containing the roast. Roll the potatoes in the fat and cook until tender and brown.

Cooking time – to parboil, 10 min.; to bake, 1 hr. (approx.)

CHRISTMAS PUDDING
(Rich, boiled)

2 cups currants	1 level tsp. mixed spice
3½ cups raisins	1 level tsp. grated nutmeg
⅓ cup sweet almonds (skinned and chopped)	5 cups bread crumbs
1 level tsp. ground ginger	2 cups finely chopped or shredded suet
2 cups plain flour	6 eggs
Pinch of salt	5 tbs. beer
2 cups brown sugar	Juice of 1 orange
1 cup mixed finely chopped candied peel	½ cup brandy
	1¼ cups milk (approx.)

Grease 3 pudding molds. Prepare the dried fruit; chop the raisins; chop the nuts.

Sift the flour, salt, spice, ginger, and nutmeg into a mixing bowl. Add the sugar, bread crumbs, suet, fruit, nuts, and candied peel. Beat the eggs well and add to them the beer, orange juice, and brandy, and stir this into the dry ingredients, adding enough milk to make the mixture of a soft dropping consistency. Put the mixture into prepared molds. Cover and boil steadily for 6-7 hr. Take the puddings out of the water and cover them with a clean, dry cloth and, when cold, store in a cool place until required.

When required, boil the puddings for 1½ hr. before serving. Serve with Brandy Butter.

3 puddings (each to give 6 medium servings)

BRANDY OR RUM SAUCE

⅝ cup light cream	5 tbs. brandy *or*
2 egg yolks	2 tbs. rum
2 tsp. brown sugar	

Mix all ingredients in a bowl. Set the bowl over a saucepan of hot water, and beat until the mixture thickens.

Rum Sauce can also be made like Brandy Butter.

BRANDY BUTTER (Hard Sauce)

6 tbs. butter	1 tsp.-1 tbs. brandy
1½ cups confectioners' sugar *or* 1 cup confectioners' sugar and ¼ cup ground almonds	1 whipped egg white (optional)

Cream the butter until soft. Sift the sugar, and cream it with the butter until white and light in texture. Mix in the almonds, if used. Work the brandy carefully into the mixture. Fold the stiffly beaten egg white into the sauce. Serve with Christmas and other steamed puddings. This sauce may be stored for several weeks in an airtight jar. It makes an excellent filling for sweet sandwiches.

FRUIT SALAD

⅜ cup sugar	1 cup green grapes
1¼ cups water	
3 oranges	1 small can pineapple segments
Rind and juice of 1 lemon	
3 ripe dessert pears	3 red-skinned dessert apples

Bring the sugar and water to a boil, together with strips of rind taken from 1 orange and the lemon. Cool. Sieve to remove the rind.

Cut up the oranges, removing the skin and white pith, and section out of the flesh, removing the seeds. Halve the grapes, removing the seeds. Place these in the cooled sugar and water. Empty the pineapple pieces and juice into the fruit salad. Refrigerate if possible.

Just before serving, quarter, core, and slice the apples thinly and toss in the lemon juice. Dice the pears and also toss in lemon juice. Add these to the fruit salad. Arrange attractively in a suitable serving dish. Chill and serve.

Fresh pineapple and canned mandarin segments are attractively colored fruit to use. Try piling the salad in a shell or half shell of pineapple. Serve with cream.

MINCE PIES

Shortcrust, Rich Shortcrust, rough puff, *or* Puff Pastry, *or* Puff Pastry, using 1½ cups flour, etc.	10-12 oz. (2-2½ cups) Mince meat Granulated or confectioners' sugar

Roll the pastry out to about ⅛-in. thickness. Cut half of it into rounds of about 2½ in. diameter and reserve these for lids. (Use a plain cutter for flaky, rough puff or Puff Pastry.) Cut the remaining pastry into rounds about 3 in. diameter and line some patty-shells. Place some Mincemeat in the shells, brush the edge of the pastry with water, and place a lid on top of each. Press the edges together well; if a plain cutter has been used, prick the edges. Brush the tops with water and sprinkle with sugar. Make a hole or 2 small cuts in the top of each. Bake in a hot oven (220-230 °C, 425-450 °F), depending on the type of pastry, for 25-30 min. Dredge tops with granulated *or* confectioners' sugar. Served hot or cold.   *8- 10 pies*

MINCEMEAT

2¼ cup cooking apples (prepared weight)	1 tsp. ground nutmeg
3 cups currants	¼ tsp. ground cloves

Christmas Cake

4½ cups seedless raisins
½ cup candied peel
1 lb. beef suet
2 cups sugar
Grated rind and juice of 2 lemons *or* 1 orange and 1 lemon
¼ tsp. ground cinnamon
½ tsp. salt
5 tbs. brandy (*see below*)

Peel and core the apples. Put these with the fruit, candied peel, and suet through the mincer. Add the other ingredients and mix well. Cover in jars and use as required.

Note: If the Mincemeat is to be used within a few days, the brandy may be omitted.

CHRISTMAS CAKE

1 cup butter *or* margarine
1 cup sugar
3 cups currants
1½ cups raisins
¾ cup glacé cherries

½ tsp. gravy brownings
2 cups flour
⅛ tsp. salt
1 tsp. mixed spice
½ tsp. baking powder
5-6 eggs
¼ cup chopped candied peel
¾ cup blanched, chopped almonds
Milk, if necessary
4-5 tsp. brandy (optional)

Line an 8-in. cake pan with waxed paper. Cream the fat and sugar until white; add gravy brownings. Sift together flour, salt, mixed spice, and baking powder. Add egg and flour alternately to the creamed fat, beating well between each addition. Stir in the prepared fruit, almonds, and (if necessary) add a little milk to make a heavy dropping consistency. Place the mixture in the cake pan and tie a piece of paper around the outside of the pan. Smooth the mixture and make a depression in the center. Bake in a warm oven (170 °C, 335 °F) for ½ hr., then reduce heat to 150 °C, 290 °F, for another 3-3½ hr. Allow to firm before removing from pan and, when cold, remove paper. Prick bottom of cake well and sprinkle brandy over it. Leave for a few days before icing.

Cooking time – 4 hr.

PETITS FOURS (1)

2 egg whites
¾ cup ground almonds
¼ cup sugar
A few drops almond extract
Rice paper
Glacé cherries
Angelica

Beat the egg whites very stiffly, and fold in gradually the mixed almonds and sugar. Drip in the almond extract as you work. Place the mixture in a pastry bag with a large decorative tube and force it onto rice paper in rosettes or oblongs. Decorate with tiny pieces of glacé cherry or angelica and bake in a moderate oven (180 °C, 350 °F) until golden brown. They take about 20 min.

20-30 small petits fours

PETITS FOURS (2)

1 square *or* oblong Genoese Cake, 1-1½ in. thick	Butter Icing and cake crumbs
Apricot marmalade *or* glaze	Almond Paste Glacé *or* Royal Icing

Cut neat shapes from the pastry: make squares, rings, triangles, and so on. Using apricot marmalade, fasten a small piece of Almond Paste *or* Butter Icing mixed with cake crumbs on top of each piece of Genoese. Coat with icing, and decorate with fine piping in scrolls, etc., as you fancy.

GENOESE CAKE

1 cup flour	½ cup sugar
Pinch of salt	6 tbs. butter *or* margarine
4 eggs	

Sift flour and salt. Beat eggs and sugar in a bowl over a pan of hot water until thick. Fold the fat into egg mixture, then fold in salted flour. Pour into lined Swiss roll pan and bake in a moderate oven (180 °C, 350 °F). When cold (after 24 hr.), cut and use as desired for small iced cakes, etc.

Cooking time – 30- 40 min.

FESTIVITY MENUS

The dishes above provide ideas for several different Christmas menus. Here is an alternative menu for a small family or for two people, which is also suitable as an Easter menu for a family. All the recipes are in this book, for this and the following two festivity menus.

For other kinds of festivity parties, such as a 4th of July outdoor party or a New Year's Eve party, pick ideas for traditional cakes at the end of this section.

CHRISTMAS OR EASTER MENU

Consommé Madrilene
*
Roast Chicken, French Style
Potato Straws   Green Peas
Tomato Salad
*
Bread Sauce   Gravy
*
Tangerine Pancakes
*
Coffee

Note: Use these pancakes for a Shrove Tuesday dinner too.

EASTER OR OTHER FESTIVAL MENU

Grapefruit Baskets
*
Crown Roast of Lamb with Saffron Rice
Steamed Cucumber Cooked Cauliflower
with White Sauce   Salad
*
Lemon or Orange Sherbet
Easter Cookies
*
Coffee
Peppermint   Creams

WINTER FESTIVITY DINNER

Cucumber Cream Soup
*
Tournedos of Beef a la Nelson
Sautéed Potatoes   Stuffed Tomatoes
Boiled French Beans   Gravy
Mixed Vegetable Salad
*
Créme Brûlée
*
Cheese and Biscuits
*
Coffee   Petits Fours

SPECIAL FESTIVAL CAKES

Here are ideas for cakes you can use on various party occasions and for some traditional festivals. Some of these cakes have a long history, and a place in the folk lore of many peoples. Gingerbreads, for instance, have been offered at festivals and fairs since pagan times and are associated with many saints' days.

CHRISTENING CAKE

Make one of the recipes for Birthday Cake and decorate it with Almond Paste and White Icing. Pipe stars or rosettes around the top edge, using pink or blue icing, according to whether the baby is a girl or boy. Pipe the baby's name in the center of the cake, in the appropriate color.

CROWN CELEBRATION CAKE

Recipe for Basic Victoria Sandwich Cake Almond Paste, using ¾ cup ground almonds Apricot Glaze	Orange glacé icing Glacé cherries, mimosa balls, etc., to decorate

Bake the Victoria Sandwich Cake in a single 8-in. ring mold for 30-40 min. Allow to cool. Make the Almond Paste. When cake has cooled, brush it with the glaze. Make the Almond Paste into 8 cones, and stand these at equal intervals around the top edge of the ring cake. Coat the cake and the cones with the icing. When it is nearly set, decorate the cake with "jewels" made from glacé cherries, etc.

MAYPOLE CHILDREN'S PARTY CAKE

Recipe for Basic Butter Sponge Cake Green glacé icing	Gaily colored pencil Narrow ribbon Small toys

Bake the Butter Sponge Cake in an 8-in. cake pan. When cold, ice the top with green icing. Insert the pencil upright in the center. To the top, attach lengths of ribbon that will reach the edge of the cake. Fasten them to the edge of the cake, at equal intervals all around it; or attach the ribbon ends to the toys and place these around the cake.

DRUM CHILDREN'S PARTY CAKE

Recipe for 2 Basic Victoria Sandwich Cakes Apricot Glaze or apricot marmalade	Recipe for 2 batches Butter Icing Brown food coloring or a little Chocolate Icing Small round yellow sweets (optional)
Recipe for 2 batches glacé icing 2 2-in. bands shiny red paper to encircle cake	

Bake the Victoria Sandwich Cakes. When cold, cut each in half horizontally. Spread the cut surfaces with Apricot Glaze or marmalade, and sandwich together again with Butter Icing. Cut off the top of 1 cake so that it is level. Brush with Apricot Glaze or marmalade, and cover with a smooth layer of Butter Icing. Place the second cake on top to make a "drum" shape. Trim any projecting edges.

Cover the cake with smooth white glacé icing. Reserve a little icing and tint it dark brown (or use Chocolate Icing if you prefer). Pipe diagonal lines from top to bottom of the cake, at intervals all around. When set, pipe similar lines slanting the opposite way, to make "diamond" outlines. Pin one band of paper around the base of the cake. Pin the other around the top, so that it stands a little higher than the cake's surface. Decorate, if desired, with small yellow candies to represent brass studs.

FAIRY COTTAGE CHILDREN'S PARTY CAKE

Recipe for Rich Dark Gingerbread Apricot Glaze Recipe for 2 batches glacé icing	Brown and green food coloring Licorice assortment and other assorted small candies

Bake the Gingerbread in 2 loaf pans the same size. Turn out, and allow to cool. When cold, trim 1 loaf into a near brick-like block. Cut through the length of the second cake, from top to bottom, diagonally, forming 2 triangular "sticks" for the roof. Brush both cakes with Apricot Glaze. Place the 2 triangular pieces "back to back" on the block, making a roof.

Ice the walls of the "cottage" with White Icing. Tint some icing brown, and ice the roof. As the icing begins to set, decorate the cake with candies for windows, door, chimneys, etc. Tint a little icing green, and spread it on the board or plate around the "cottage" to represent grass.

HALLOWE'EN PARTY CAKE

Recipe for	Chocolate finger
Basic Victoria	cookies
Sandwich Cake	A little glacé
Recipe for 2	icing tinted red
batches Chocolate	Red foil paper
Butter Icing	Cotton wool
Cocoa	

Make the Victoria Sandwich Cake in a 1½-qt. mold pan. Cool on a wire rack.

When cold, ice with the Chocolate Butter Icing, and scatter a little sieved cocoa over it. Dust the finger cookies with cocoa, and pile them up around the cake to make it look like a bonfire. Drip on red glacé icing to represent small flames, and add cotton wool for "smoke."

YULE LOG CHRISTMAS CAKE

Recipe for	White glacé
Chocolate Swiss	icing
Roll	Almond Paste
Recipe for	tinted green or
Chocolate	angelica
Butter Icing	Small round
Cocoa	red candies

Make the Chocolate Swiss Roll as described, but fill with Chocolate Butter Icing instead of vanilla. Dust the outside of the "log" with cocoa, and decorate with lines of white glacé icing, to represent snow. Cut holly leaves from tinted Almond Paste or angelica, add candies for berries, and use to decorate the cake.

If you wish, make 2 small extra Chocolate Swiss Rolls, and use them as side "branches" for the "log."

EASTER-EGG CAKE

Recipe for 2	Small quantity
Basic Victoria	brown food
Sandwich Cakes	coloring (if
Apricot Glaze	glacé icing is
or apricot	used) or
marmalade	Chocolate Icing
Recipe for	Small yellow
Almond Paste,	chicks and 1
using 1½ cups	larger chick
ground almonds	
or recipe for	
2 batches	
Coffee Icing	

Bake the Victoria Sandwich Cakes in 2 1½-qt. mold pans. Turn out and cool on wire racks. When cold, stand 1 cake upright on its smaller end. Cut off the top, if necessary, so that it is level. Brush the cake all over with Apricot Glaze or marmalade. Cover the sides with a smooth layer of Almond Paste or Coffee Icing. Cut the larger flat surface of the second cake so that it stands level. Brush with Apricot Glaze or marmalade. Invert the cake onto the first cake to make an egg shape. Brush the top and sides of the second cake with Apricot Glaze or marmalade.

Carefully cut a small slice from the narrow top of the cake on top, leaving it attached at one side. Scoop out a very small amount of cake from underneath the cut slice. Brush the cut surfaces with Apricot Glaze or marmalade. Then cover this top cake with Almond Paste or icing like the bottom one, including both sides of the cut slice and the inside of the scooped-out portion. Prop up the cut slice with a pencil while the icing sets. When it is set, pipe a line of dark-tinted icing or Chocolate Icing around the edge of the cut slice, and place the largest chick inside the scooped-out "shell," propping up the cut slice. Stand the smaller chicks around the base of the cake.

MOTHER'S CAKE
To be served on Mother's Day

Mixture: as for Birthday Cake baked in a 6-in. pan.
Almond Paste, using 1 cup ground almonds, etc.

Royal Icing, using 3 cups confectioners' sugar, etc.

Cover cake with Almond Paste and allow to dry. Pour over Royal Icing of coating consistency — make as smooth as possible and remove blisters with a pin or skewer; allow to firm before decorating. Place the cake on a cake dish 1 in. larger than the cake. Pipe a circle around the top rim of the cake with a ¼-in. plain tube. Allow to set, then pipe a second circle on top of the first; repeat a third time (but use a small plain tube) and a fourth, if fancied. Pipe in the same way on the base. Make some yellow or red roses and some green leaves from colored Almond Paste and use to decorate the top. Pipe on the words "Mother's Day."

SIMNEL CAKE

Mixture: as for Birthday Cake or any other fruit cake
Almond Paste:
1 cup almonds, etc.
Glacé Icing: ½ cup confectioners' sugar, etc.

Line a 6- or 7-in. cake-pan. Cut off about ⅓ of the Almond Paste and roll out into a round slightly less than the diameter of the pan to be used. Place ½ the cake mixture in the pan, cover with a round of Almond Paste, and place the remaining cake mixture on top. Bake in a moderate oven (180 °C, 350 °F) for ½ hr.; reduce heat to cool (140-150 °C, 275-300 °F) for 2-2½ hr. Leave for 24 hr. Using about ½ the remaining Almond Paste, cover the top of the cake. With the remainder, make small balls and place these at even intervals around the top edge of the cake. Brush them over with egg wash. Tie a band of waxed paper tightly around the top of the cake. Place in a hot oven until the balls are nicely browned. When cool, pour glacé icing into the center of the cake and decorate as required with almond-paste eggs, small chicks, etc.

This cake used to be served on Mother's Day but is now usually served on Easter Sunday.

Cooking time – about 3 hr.

TWELFTH NIGHT CAKE

¾ cup butter *or* margarine	½ cup mixed candied peel
⅜ cup brown sugar	½ level tsp. ground cinnamon
3 eggs	½ level tsp. mixed spice
5 tbs. milk	3 cups flour
1 level tsp. soda	¼ tsp. salt
¼ cup molasses	
¾ cup currants	
¾ cup raisins	

Line a 7-in. cake pan with waxed paper. Cream the fat and sugar and beat in the eggs gradually. Add the milk in which the soda is dissolved; stir in the molasses and beat well. Add the prepared fruit and spices. Sift in the flour and salt and mix lightly. Put into the pan and bake in a warm oven (175 °C, 335 °F). Silver charms should be baked in the cake; wrap in waxed paper.

Cooking time – 2- 2½ hr.

VALENTINE'S CAKE

6 tbs. butter *or* margarine	2 eggs
⅜ cup sugar	1 cup self-rising flour
Grated rind of lemon *or* orange	Pinch of salt

Decoration:

Glacé icing using 3 cups confectioners' sugar, etc.	Red Almond Paste
	Green *or* chocolate Almond Paste

Grease and dust with flour a heart-shaped pan 7 in. wide, shaking out any surplus flour. Cream fat and sugar until white, and beat in the lemon or orange rind. Add the eggs one at a time and beat each until the mixture is very light. Sift the flour and salt and fold into the mixture. Put the mixture into the pan. Bake in a moderate oven (180 °C, 350 °F) for ¾-1 hr. Allow to cool for a few minutes, then turn out.

When cold, coat the cake with the glacé icing and, when the icing is firm enough — not too dry — decorate with two heart shapes cut out of red Almond Paste. Make an arrow of chocolate *or* green Almond Paste and place it to look as if it goes through the hearts.

RICH DARK GINGERBREAD

2 cups flour	2-4 oz. crystallized ginger
⅛ tsp. salt	
1-2 tsp ground cinnamon	⅓ cup blanched, chopped almonds
1-2 tsp. mixed spice	½ cup butter *or* margarine
2 tsp. ground ginger	½ cup sugar
⅓ cup dates *or* raisins	½ cup molasses
1 tsp. soda	2 eggs
	A little warm milk, if required

Grease a 7-in. pan and line the bottom with well greased waxed paper.

Mix flour, salt, and other dry ingredients with the prepared fruit, crystallized ginger cut into pieces, and almonds. Melt the fat, sugar, and molasses; add to the dry ingredients with the beaten eggs. If the mixture seems stiff, add a little warm milk, but do not make it too soft. Pour into the pan, and bake in a warm-to-cool oven (150-170 °C, 310-335 °F).

Cooking time – 1¾ hr.- 2 hr.

HOT CROSS BUNS

4 cups flour	1 tbs. yeast
½ tsp. salt	1-2 eggs
¼ cup margarine *or* margarine and lard	1-1¼ cups milk
	⅓ cup currants *or* ⅓ cup raisins and peel
½ cup sugar	
1 tsp. mixed spice *or* cinnamon	Shortcrust Pastry trimmings

Mix salt with warmed flour. Rub in fat. Add sugar, spice, creamed yeast, and eggs with the warm milk. Mix to a soft, light dough, beat well, and let rise. When well-risen, knead the dough lightly, working in the fruit, and divide into 20-24 pieces. Form into round shapes, flatten slightly, and let stand for 15 min. Cut narrow strips of pastry 1½-2 in. long, brush tops of buns with egg wash *or* milk, place pastry crosses on top, and bake in a hot oven (220 °C, 425 °F).

20- 24 buns   Cooking time – 15- 20 min.

BLACK BUN FOR A SCOTS' NEW YEAR'S EVE

PASTRY

4 cups flour	⅝ cup butter *or*
¼ tsp. salt	margarine
¾ level tsp.	Water to mix
baking powder	

Filling:

6 cups currants	1 tsp. ground
6 cups raisins	ginger
⅓ cup glacé	1 tsp. allspice
cherries	1 tsp. black
¼ cup chopped	pepper
peel	2 level tsp.
1 cup blanched,	soda
chopped	2 level tsp.
almonds	cream of tartar
1 cup sugar	1 egg
3 cups flour	Milk to bind
2 level tsp.	
ground cinnamon	

Make the pastry: sift flour, salt, and baking powder, rub in the margarine, and mix with water to a stiff dough.

Mix prepared fruit and nuts with flour, sugar, spices, and rising agents for the filling; add the egg and milk to mix stiffly.

Line a greased 7- or 8-in. cake pan with ⅔ of the pastry; put in the mixture and make level; wet the edges. Roll out the remaining ⅓ of pastry, place on top, and smooth the edges. Prick well all over the top, brush with egg, and bake in a very cool oven (150 °C, 300°F).

Cooking time – 4- 5 hr.

FESTIVE GATEAU

½ cup flour	1 oz. grated
4 large eggs	Bournville
¼ cup ground	chocolate
hazelnuts	2 tbs. butter,
	melted

Filling and Decoration:

2 oz. Bournville	1 level tbs.
chocolate	sifted
⅝ cup heavy	confectioners'
cream	sugar

Grease and line 2 7-in. baking pans, twice. Beat the eggs and sugar together. Gently stir in the chocolate and flour. Fold in the melted butter; divide the mixture evenly between the pans and bake in a moderate oven, 180 °C, 350 °F, for 20 min.

To complete the cake, roast the hazelnuts in a hot oven for 2-3 min., then remove skins by rubbing in a cloth. Break the chocolate and put into a bowl standing over a pan of hot water until melted. Let cool. Whip the cream; fold in the confectioners' sugar alternately with the cooled chocolate and sandwich the cakes together with half the chocolate cream, then spread the remainder over the top. Decorate with a fork.

ICEBOX CAKE

1½ cups	2 tbs. lemon
confectioners'	juice
sugar	48 ladyfingers
½ cup butter	
2 medium eggs	
2 tsp. grated	
lemon peel	

Cream butter and sugar until light and fluffy, and work in eggs 1 at a time. Gradually add lemon peel and juice and beat hard until fluffy and smooth. Cover a piece of cardboard with foil and on it place 12 ladyfingers, curved side down. Spread on ⅓ of creamed mixture. Put another layer of ladyfingers in opposite direction, and more creamed mixture. Repeat layers and end with a layer of ladyfingers. Wrap in foil and chill in the refrigerator for several hours. To serve, leave at room temperature for 1 hr. Then unwrap and cover with whipped cream.

Children's Parties

Small children love a party, especially a birthday party. Colorful small cakes and other foods appeal to them, although they like them to be familiar, something they know. They like savories too, more than we sometimes realize. All food for small children should be in small portions and easy to eat without making a mess.

SAUSAGE SNACKS

Cooked whole or halved, small sausages make attractive snacks when brightly garnished. Halve sausages crosswise and set each, cut side down, on a small toasted croute. Spear whole sausages on wooden cocktail picks, and stick these into a large grapefruit or small melon with a thin slice cut from the bottom so that it stands level. Top sausages with maraschino cherries, pickled onions, cheese cubes, and chunks of canned pineapple.

Hot dogs or Vienna sausages can be treated in the same way, or can be split lengthwise and filled with cream cheese before being speared on cocktail sticks.

POTATO CRISPS

6 egg-sized potatoes	Deep fat Salt

Scrub and rinse the potatoes. Slice very thinly with a sharp knife or on a potato slicer. Drop them into cold water as they are cut. Drain, rinse, and dry them well between the folds of a clean cloth. Sprinkle gradually into hot deep fat (320 °F) and fry until golden and crisp. Remove from the fat as they brown and drain on absorbent paper. Keep them hot while frying the rest. Sprinkle with salt. They can be kept in an airtight tin for some time and be reheated when necessary.

Note: To the professional cook or chef these are known as "chips." They are served with steaks and chops and with poultry and game but may also be served with many meat and fish dishes.

6 servings   Cooking time – 3- 4 min.

SAUSAGE ROLLS

Rough Puff Pastry using 1 cup flour, etc.	½ lb. sausages Egg yolk to glaze

Roll out the pastry and cut into 8 even-sized squares. Skin the sausages. Divide the sausage meat into 8 portions and make each piece into a roll the same length as the pastry. Place the sausage meat on the pastry, wet the edge, and fold over, leav-

53

Sausage Rolls

Sausage Snacks

ing the ends open. Secure the edges with the back of a knife. Make 3 incisions on top. Brush over with beaten egg and place on a baking sheet. Bake in a hot oven (220 °C, 425 °F) until the pastry is well risen and brown. Reduce the heat and continue baking until the pastry is cooked.

Note: Small Sausage Rolls can be made quickly by rolling the pastry into an oblong. Form the sausage meat into long rolls the length of the pastry, place the meat on the pastry, then divide the pastry into strips wide enough to encircle the meat. Dampen one edge of each strip, fold over, and press together firmly. Cut into rolls of the desired length; finish as above.

Homemade sausage "spiral" rolls are a decorative alternative. Use whole small sausages with skins. Roll out the pastry into a long strip about ½ in. wide. Wrap pastry strip diagonally around each sausage, leaving a small gap between strip edges. Bake as above.

8 sausage rolls   Cooking time – about ½ hr.

SMALL PLAIN CAKES

For Small Plain Cakes, use the variations suggested under Basic Plain Buns. Small "butter sponge" cakes can be cut from a Basic Butter Sponge or Victoria Sandwich Cake baked in a square or oblong pan. For small sponge cakes and rich cakes use the mixture below. The Butterfly Orange Cakes are particularly attractive for a children's party.

BASIC SMALL SPONGE CAKES

¾ cup flour	1 level tsp.
Pinch of salt	baking powder
3 eggs	½ tsp. vanilla
⅜ cup sugar	extract

Make like the Basic Large Sponge Cake. Put the mixture into oblong sponge cake pans prepared by greasing and dusting with equal quantities of flour and sugar.

54

Small Butterflies

Half-fill the pans and dredge the tops with sugar. Bake in a moderate oven (170-180 °C, 325-350 °F) until well risen, firm, and a pale fawn color.

10-12 cakes   Cooking time – 20 min.

BASIC SMALL "RICH" CAKES

The following is a suitable mixture for all these small cakes and can be varied in many ways.

BASIC RECIPE

¼ cup butter *or* margarine	Pinch of salt
¼ cup sugar	Water *or* milk
1 egg	as required
¾ cup self-rising flour *or* ¾ cup plain flour and 1 tsp. baking powder	

Beat the fat and sugar until creamy and white. Beat the egg and add gradually; beat well between each addition. Sift together the flour, salt, and baking powder. Gently stir the flour, etc., into the creamed fat; add milk or water to make a soft dropping consistency. Half-fill greased muffin pans with the mixture and bake in a fairly hot to moderate oven (180-190 °C, 350-375 °F).

Note: This mixture can be baked in paper cupcake cases and decorated with glacé icing or cherries.

10 - 12 cakes   Cooking time – 15 - 20 min.

VARIATIONS OF BASIC RECIPE

Cherry Cakes
Add ¼-½ cup coarsely chopped glacé cherries with the flour.

Chocolate Cakes
Sift 2 tbs. cocoa with the flour, and add a few drops of vanilla extract with the water or milk. The cakes can be iced with Chocolate Icing.

Coconut Cakes
Add ½ oz. coconut with the flour and add ¼ tsp. vanilla extract with the milk or water.

Lemon or Orange Cakes
Add the grated rind of 1 lemon or orange with the flour, and ice with Lemon or Orange Icing.

Madeleines
Bake the basic mixture in greased dariole or castle pudding molds. Turn out when baked, cool. Spread all around, top and sides, with warmed apricot jam. Roll in desiccated coconut and decorate with ½ glacé cherry.

Nut Cakes
Add ¼-½ cup coarsely chopped walnuts, almonds, or hazelnuts with the flour.

Queen Cakes
Add ¼-½ cup currants *or* raisins with the flour, or a few currants may be placed in the bottom of each queen cake pan and the mixture placed on top.

BUTTERFLY ORANGE CAKES

The basic mixture for Small Rich Cakes, flavored with orange and cooked in greased bouchée pans
⅝ cup sweetened cream, flavored with orange liqueur *or* extract
A little apricot jam

Cut a thin slice from the top of each cake. Cut each slice in 2, to make 2 wings. Dredge with confectioners' sugar. Spread the cut top of each cake with a little jam, pipe a rosette of whipped cream on this, and place the wings in position.

10 - 12 cakes

BASIC COOKIE RECIPE
(Shrewsbury Cookies)

½ cup butter *or* margarine	½ tsp. ground cinnamon
½ cup sugar	*or* 1 tsp. grated lemon rind
1 small egg	
2 cups flour	Milk as required

Cream the fat and sugar and beat in the egg. Sift flour with cinnamon, *or* add grated rind, and add to the creamed fat mixture. Mix to a stiff consistency, using milk if required. Roll out fairly thin and cut out with a 2½-in. cutter. Place on a greased baking sheet and bake in a moderate oven (180 °C, 350 °F) until light fawn color.
30 - 32 cookies   Cooking time – 15 - 20 min.

EASTER COOKIES

Add ½ level tsp. mixed spice and ½ cup currants to the basic recipe for Shrewsbury Cookies. Roll out mixture to ¼ in. thickness and cut into 4-in. rounds. If desired, brush with egg white and dredge with sugar. Bake in a moderate oven (180 °C, 350 °F) until golden brown.
12 - 16 cookies   Cooking time – 20 - 30 min.

ANIMAL COOKIES

Use the Basic Cookie Recipe, cut out with an animal-shaped cutter; decorate with faces in Chocolate or Coffee Icing.

MELTING MOMENTS

¼ cup lard *or* hydrogenated shortening	½ tsp. vanilla extract
¼ cup margarine	1¼ cups self-rising flour
⅜ cup sugar	Cornflakes
½ egg	

Cream fat and sugar and beat in egg. Add flavoring, stir in the sifted flour, and, with wet hands, make into balls the size of marbles and roll in crushed cornflakes. Bake in a fairly hot to moderate oven (180-190 °C, 350-375 °F).

24 cookies   Cooking time – 15 min.

GINGERSNAPS

1½ cups self-rising flour	⅜-½ cup sugar
Pinch of salt	¼ cup lard *or* shortening
1 tsp. soda	1½ tbs. corn syrup
2 tsp. ground ginger	1 egg

Note: Take small measure of soda and ginger.

Sift flour, salt, soda, and ginger; add sugar. Melt lard and syrup, cool slightly, then add to dry ingredients; add the egg. Divide into 24 pieces and make into balls; place well apart on greased baking sheets. Bake in a fairly hot to moderate oven (180-190 °C, 350-375 °F) until a good rich brown color.

24 Gingersnaps   Cooking time – 20 min.

COCONUT PYRAMIDS

3 egg whites	½ tsp. vanilla extract
⅜ rice flour	Rice paper
½-⅝ cup sugar	
8 oz. desiccated coconut	

Beat the egg whites very stiffly; stir in the rice flour, sugar, coconut, and vanilla. Put the mixture in small close heaps on rice paper; bake in a cool oven (150 °C, 300 °F) until they are light brown.

18 pyramids

BIRTHDAY CAKE
(FRUIT and BUTTER SPONGE)

Ingredients for Fruit Cake

½ cup butter *or* margarine	2 cups mixed fruit — raisins, currants, glacé cherries
½ cup brown sugar	
1½ tbs. corn syrup	¼ cup candied peel *or* marmalade
2 eggs	
1½ cups plain flour	¼ cup milk (approx.)
⅛ tsp. salt	
1 level tsp. baking powder	
1 tsp. mixed spice	

For the older child, a birthday cake can be a fruit cake.

Line a 6-7-in. cake pan. Cream fat, sugar, and syrup thoroughly. Beat eggs and add alternately with the sifted flour, salt, and baking powder, beating well with each addition. Add remaining ingredients and fruit, which has been mixed with a little of the flour. Mix to a fairly soft consistency with milk and place in the cake pan. Bake for ½ hr. in a moderate oven (180 °C, 390 °F) and another 2-2½ hr. in a cool oven (140-150 °C, 275-300 °F).

For a younger child, a "butter sponge" birthday cake is more suitable than a fruit cake. A most attractive cake can be made from enough of the Basic Butter Sponge Cake mixture to fill 3 7-in. cake pans. One-third of the mixture should be colored with a few drops of food coloring before being put in its pan; after baking, it should be "sandwiched" between the other two layers, to make a colored layer between them.

A fruit cake is usually coated with Almond Paste and decorated with Royal Icing. A sponge cake can be decorated most successfully with a Butter Icing, or Boiled White Icing.

Cooking time – about 3 hr. (fruit cake); 40 min. (butter sponge)

Birthday Cake

of a spoon thickly. Pour quickly over the cake. Spread with a spatula, and work up the icing in swirls. You can also use the icing as a filling. One-half tsp. vanilla extract or lemon juice and a pinch of cream of tartar are the most usual additions. For other flavorings, see Butter Icings.

FUDGE

2 cups sugar	½ tsp. vanilla
5/8 cup milk	extract
¼ cup butter	

Put sugar and milk in a saucepan and let soak for 1 hr. Add the butter, place over low heat and stir until sugar is dissolved. Then bring to a boil and boil to the soft-ball stage (237 °F). Remove from heat, stir in vanilla, cool slightly, then beat until thick. Pour into greased pan; cut in squares when cold.

Note: Coconut, nuts, or ginger may be stirred in while fudge is cooling. **Chocolate Fudge:** Add 2 tbs. cocoa or 2 oz. plain chocolate with the butter.

BASIC BUTTER SPONGE CAKE

½ cup butter *or*	Pinch salt
margarine	1 tsp. baking
¾ cup sugar	powder
4 eggs	4 tsp. cold water
1½ cups self-	to mix
rising flour	

Make like a Victoria Sandwich Cake.

BOILED WHITE ICING

1 cup sugar	1 egg white,
4 tbs. water	beaten
	with flavoring

Put the sugar and water into a pan. Dissolve the sugar slowly in the water, then bring to boiling point. Boil to 130 °C, 240 °F, without stirring. Brush down the sides of the pan with a brush dipped in cold water, and remove scum as it rises. Pour onto the beaten egg white and flavoring, beating all the time. Continue beating until the icing begins to thicken and coats the back

BUTTER ICING OR BUTTER CREAM FILLING (1) (quick)

¼ cup butter *or*	Flavoring
margarine	Pinch of salt
¾ cup	Coloring
confectioners'	
sugar	

Cream the butter or margarine. Add the confectioners' sugar and salt gradually and cream together. Beat until smooth, creamy, and pale. Add flavoring and coloring to taste.

FLAVORINGS

Almond Beat in ¼ tsp. almond extract.

Chocolate Dissolve 1 oz. chocolate in 1 tbs. water and beat in, *or* beat in 2 tsp. cocoa and a few drops of vanilla extract.

Coffee Beat in 2 tsp. liquid coffee.

Jam Add 1 tbs. strong-flavored jam, e.g. plum, raspberry.

Lemon Beat in 1 tsp. strained lemon juice.

Orange Beat in 2 tsp. strained orange juice.

Vanilla Beat in ½ tsp. vanilla extract.

Walnut Add ½ cup chopped walnuts and 1-2 tsp. liquid coffee.

In cold weather, you may warm the butter slightly, but do not let it oil. This butter icing always has a slight taste of raw sugar. A better but more costly one is made thus:

BUTTER ICING OR BUTTER CREAM (2)

½-¾ cup sugar	unsalted butter (for icing)
4 egg yolks	
⅝ cup milk	
½ cup unsalted butter (for filling) *or* 1 cup	Flavoring as above

59

Beat the egg yolks until fluffy; then beat in the sugar gradually until the mixture is thick and very pale. Heat the milk and, when at boiling point, trickle it into the egg yolk mixture, beating all the time. Return the mixture to the milk saucepan and heat it gently until it thickens. Place the saucepan in a pan of cold water to cool; cover, and beat often enough to prevent a skin forming. When the custard is tepid, beat in the flavoring and butter alternately. Chill if a stiff icing is desired.

MARSHMALLOWS

¼ lb. gum arabic	3 egg whites
1¼ cups water	Caramel flavoring
2 cups confectioners' sugar	

Soak the gum arabic in the water until soft, then heat gently until dissolved, and strain it through fine muslin. Return to the pan, add the sugar, and, when dissolved, stir in the egg whites, and beat until the mixture is quite stiff. Flavor to taste, and let it remain for about 10 hr. When ready, cut into small squares and dredge them thickly with confectioners' sugar.

NOUGAT

| 1½ cups almonds | ⅜ cup honey |
| 1 cup confectioners' sugar | 2 egg whites |

Blanch and dry the almonds thoroughly. Line an 8×8-in. square pan with white paper and then with wafer paper, both of which must be cut to fit exactly. Put the sugar, honey, and egg whites into a sugar boiler or saucepan, and stir over a low heat until the mixture becomes thick and white. Drop a little into cold water; if it hardens immediately, remove the pan from the heat and stir in the almonds. Dredge the slab with confectioners' sugar, turn onto it the nougat, and form into a ball. Press into the prepared pan, cover with paper, let it sit until cold, then cut into squares.

Teenagers' Parties

DEVILS ON HORSEBACK

1-2 chickens' livers *or* 3-4 oz. calf's liver	8 short thin slices bacon
Butter	4 small bread squares
Salt and pepper	Olives stuffed
Cayenne pepper	with pimiento
8 well-drained prunes, cooked	

Gently cook the liver in a little butter, then cut it into 8 pieces. Season well and dust with a few grains of cayenne pepper. Stone the prunes and stuff with the liver. Stretch the bacon to double its size with the flat of a knife. Encircle each prune in a piece of bacon, secure with a wooden cocktail stick, and bake in a very hot oven. Fry the bread in shallow bacon fat and drain well. Remove sticks and place the "devils" on the bread. Garnish each with a pimiento-stuffed olive.

KEDGEREE

1 lb. cold cooked fish (smoked haddock is generally preferred)	2 hard-boiled eggs
	¼ cup butter
	Salt and pepper
⅝ cup rice	Cayenne pepper

Boil and dry the rice. Divide the fish into small flakes. Cut the whites of the eggs into slices and sieve the yolks. Melt the butter in a saucepan, add to it the fish, rice, egg whites, salt, pepper, and cayenne and stir until hot. Turn the mixture onto a hot dish. With a fork, press into the shape of a pyramid, decorate with egg yolk, and serve as hot as possible.

5-6 servings   Cooking time – 40-50 min.

BACON OLIVES

½ cup finely chopped cooked *or* canned meat	½ tsp. finely chopped parsley
	¼ tsp. powdered mixed herbs
3 tbs. finely chopped cooked ham *or* tongue	Nutmeg
	Salt and pepper
1½ tbs. bread crumbs	1 egg
	8 small thin slices of bacon
½ tsp. finely chopped onion	

Mix the meat, ham, bread crumbs, onion, parsley, and herbs together, add a pinch of nutmeg; season to taste with salt and pepper. Stir in gradually as much egg as is necessary to bind the mixture together. Leave for ½ hr., then divide into 8 portions. Form each portion into a cork shape, roll in a slice of bacon, and secure with string or small skewers. Bake in a fairly hot

61

Seafood Flan

Brandy Snaps

Apple Loaf

Stuffed Ham Rolls

oven (190 °C, 375 °F) for about ½ hr. Serve on toast.

SEAFOOD FLAN

| ¼ cup butter or margarine | 2 tbs. grated cheese |
| ¼ tsp. salt | 1⅓ cups crushed plain crackers |

Filling:

2 tsp. gelatin	1 tsp. finely chopped onion
½ 3-oz. can pink salmon or tuna	1 tsp. finely chopped parsley
6 sardines	Salt and pepper to taste
⅝ cup mayonnaise	
2 tbs. tomato ketchup	

To make the flan case: cream fat, salt, and cheese together and knead in the crushed crackers. Place mixture on a plate and mold it into a greased 7-in flan ring. Put into refrigerator until firmly set. Remove flan ring.

Dissolve gelatin in 3 tbs. hot water. Flake the salmon or tuna and sardines (free from bones) and mix together all ingredients for filling. When beginning to set, pour into prepared flan case. Decorate with hard-boiled egg and shelled shrimps.

BAKED AND STUFFED POTATOES

6 large potatoes

Stuffing, choice of:

1) ¾ cup grated cheese; 2 tbs. butter or margarine; a little milk; seasoning; nutmeg

2) ¾ cup chopped, fried bacon; a little milk; seasoning

3) ¾ cup mashed, cooked smoked haddock; chopped parsley; lemon juice; a little milk; nutmeg

4) 2 boned kippers, cooked and mashed; a little milk

5) ½ cup grated cheese; 2 tbs. butter; chopped parsley; a little milk; season-ing; 2 egg yolks stirred into the filling; 2 egg whites folded in at the end

6) ¾ cup ground beef; ½ small minced onion and seasoning; all sautéed and mixed

Scrub, rinse, and dry the potatoes, then grease them. With a small sharp knife, cut through the skin of the potatoes to give the appearance of a lid. Bake for 1-1½ hr. at 190 °C, 375 °F. Lift off lids carefully, scoop out cooked potatoes from skins, including lids, taking care not to split the skins. Mash the potatoes in a bowl and add the ingredients of any one of the stuffings listed above. Mix well and season thoroughly. Fill the potato skins with the mixture, piling it high. Fork the tops and brush with a little egg, or sprinkle with a little grated cheese (if an ingredient of the stuffing). Put back in the oven and bake until thoroughly hot and golden brown. Serve in a hot dish garnished with parsley and with the skin "lids" replaced, if liked.

Note: A stuffing consisting of cooked minced meat in a sauce or gravy or of cooked mixed vegetables or flaked fish in a sauce may replace the floury meal of the potato entirely. The latter should then be mashed and served separately or mashed and piped around the opening of the potato after it has been stuffed and before returning it to the oven.

6 servings   Cooking time – about 2 hr.

HAMBURGERS

1 lb. ground beef	Salt and pepper
½ cup dry bread crumbs	1 small onion, minced
½ cup milk	

Mix all ingredients together. Form mixture into 6 patties, brown quickly on both sides in hot fat, reduce heat, and cook more slowly until done, turning occasionally. Serve in round, split, toasted rolls.

HAM ROLLS

| 4 thin slices of cooked ham | 1-2 tbs. sweet chutney |
| 2 oz. cream cheese | Crisp lettuce |

Spread each slice of ham on a board; trim

off surplus fat. Mix the cream cheese and chutney together, spread over the ham and roll. Put onto lettuce leaves. If desired, cut the slices into 1-in. lengths and instead of putting onto lettuce leaves put on small buttered biscuits and garnish with watercress leaves.

4 servings or 12 small snacks

PARTY SKEWERS

Make a mixed grill with sausage, kidney, liver, mushroom, bacon rolls, small onion rings, and small squares of fried bread. Cut the pieces of food into small 1-in. pieces when cooked, leaving the bacon rolls whole. Have ready some clean wooden orange sticks and arrange 4 or 5 pieces of food on each stick. Keep the food hot until served.

CHICKEN VOL-AU-VENT

1¼ cups cooked chicken	2-4 mushrooms
Puff Pastry,	Salt, pepper,
frozen *or* using	nutmeg
2 cups flour, etc.	1¼ cups
⅓ cup cooked	Béchamel
ham *or* tongue	Sauce
½ cup cooked	Egg *or* milk
noodles	to glaze

Prepare the pastry; roll out to ¾ in. thick. Cut into a round or oval shape and place on a wet baking sheet. Cut an inner ring through half the depth of the pastry and brush top of pastry (not sides) with beaten egg. Bake in a hot oven (220-230 °C, 425-450 °F) until well-risen, firm, and brown (about 25 min.). Dice chicken and ham, slice mushrooms; add these with the noodles to the Béchamel Sauce, season well, and heat thoroughly. Lift center from vol-au-vent shell and reserve for lid, clear any soft paste that may be inside, fill with the mixture, and replace lid.

A separate piece of pastry the size of the lid may be baked with the large shell and used as a lid for the filled shell; this has a better appearance.

Alternatively, make the pastry into 6 individual shells, and use the following filling:

Filling:

1 10½-oz. can condensed cream of mushroom soup	⅓ cup cooked ham, diced
	1-2 tbs. cream (optional)
2 cups cooked chicken *or* turkey meat, diced	

Heat the chicken and ham in the soup, then add the cream, if used. Fill the prepared cases. Put them into a preheated moderate oven (180 °C, 350 °F) to warm through and crisp. Serve hot or cold, with a crisp salad.

6 servings

SAUSAGES (COCKTAIL, FRANKFURTER, AND LARGE)

Cocktail Sausages are best baked. Separate the sausages, prick them with a fork, and lay them in a baking pan. Bake without extra fat at 180 °C, 350 °F, for about 10 min., until brown on top. Turn, and bake 7-10 min. longer to brown the underneath.

Frankfurters are treated like large sausages (*see* below). Alternatively, they can be pricked and simmered in white wine with a pinch of thyme until tender (about 10 min.).

Large sausages Prick large sausages first with a fork, throw into boiling water, and simmer for 15 min. Put into a frying pan containing a little hot fat, and fry gently, turning to brown all sides. To fry large sausages, heat slowly to prevent the sausages bursting.

SAUSAGE AND APPLE MASH

½ lb. sausages	Pinch of curry powder
3 tomatoes, halved	1 tsp. lemon juice
3 medium potatoes	Salt and pepper
2 tbs. butter	Chopped parsley
⅝ cup Apple Sauce	

Fry the sausages gently until brown all

65

Macaroni au Gratin with Bacon Rolls

over and cooked thoroughly. Add the tomatoes to the pan and cook gently. Meanwhile, boil the potatoes, drain, and mash well. Add the butter, heated Apple Sauce, curry powder, lemon juice, and seasoning and mix well. Spoon or pipe onto a warm serving dish, arrange the sausages and tomatoes on top, and decorate with parsley.

Alternatively, omit the tomatoes, and instead of adding Apple Sauce to the potatoes, use plain mashed potatoes and add grilled apple slices to the dish as a garnish.

2 servings

MEATBALLS

1 small onion	1 tsp. potato
A little lard	flour
4 oz. ground	1½ tsp. salt
beef	¼ tsp. white
2½ oz. pork	pepper
1-1½ cups milk	1 tsp. sugar
1 egg	1-2 tbs. butter
2 tbs. bread	or cream
crumbs	(optional)

Peel, slice, and fry onions slightly in a little lard. Wash meat and pass 3 times through mincer, together with the fried onion, or blend in an electric blender for a few seconds. Mix milk and egg; soak bread crumbs and flour in this, add salt, pepper, sugar, cream or butter (if used), and, finally the meat. Mix well. Make into small balls and brown in butter or fat.

Meatballs are a favorite dish in Sweden and can be eaten fried or boiled with potato salad with various sauces: mushroom and tomato, etc.

4 servings

CHEESE AND ONION PIE

Shortcrust	2 tbs. flour
Pastry, frozen *or*	Salt and pepper
using 2 cups	1 cup grated
flour, etc., if	cheese
homemade	2 tbs. milk
3 small onions	

Parboil the onions while making the pastry.

Line an 8-in. pie pan with half the pastry.

Sausage and Apple Mash

Mix the salt and pepper with the flour. Slice the onions and dip in the seasoned flour; spread them over the bottom of the lined plate. Grate the cheese and sprinkle it over the onion; add the milk. Wet the edge of the pastry, put on the cover, and press the edges firmly together. Secure the edges, decorate as desired, and brush over with milk. Bake in a hot oven (220 °C, 425 °F) for about 40 min.

This can be made as an open tart if liked, using 1 cup flour, etc., for the pastry.

6 - 8 servings

SCOTCH EGGS

3 hard-boiled eggs	Egg and bread crumbs
½ lb. sausage meat	Frying fat

Shell the eggs and cover each with sausage meat. If liked, a little finely chopped onion can be mixed with the sausage meat before using. Coat carefully with beaten egg and bread crumbs; fry in hot fat until nicely browned. Cut each egg in half. Scotch eggs can be served either hot or cold.

3 servings

CHEESE FLAN

Cheese Pastry:	Filling:
2 cups flour	1 egg
Pinch of salt and cayenne pepper	⅝ cup milk
½ cup butter	¾ cup grated cheddar cheese
1 cup grated cheddar cheese	Pinch of salt
1 egg yolk	A few grains cayenne pepper
Little cold water to mix	

Sift flour and seasonings into a bowl. Rub in the butter until mixture resembles fine bread crumbs. Stir in cheese, and bind together with egg yolk and water. Roll out on a floured board to ¼-in. thick and line a greased flan pan, approx. 8 in. long and 1 in. deep. Prick with a fork and bake in a fairly hot oven (200 °C, 400 °F) for 20 min. Cool, and remove flan from tin.

To make the filling, beat together the egg, milk, most of the grated cheese, and the seasoning. Pour into flan shell, sprinkle with the remaining cheese, and bake in a fairly hot oven (200 °C, 400 °F) for about 20 min., until the top is golden brown. Serve hot.

4 servings

MACARONI AU GRATIN WITH BACON ROLLS

1 cup macaroni	Browned bread crumbs *or*
2½ cups White Sauce	¼ cup finely grated cheddar cheese
1 cup grated cheese	
Bacon slices	Butter
Salt and pepper	

Put the macaroni into rapidly boiling salted water and boil for about 20 min., or until tender. (If not required for immediate use, cover the macaroni with cold water to prevent the pieces sticking together.) Cover the bottom of a well-buttered baking dish with White Sauce, sprinkle liberally with cheese, seasoning to taste, and add a layer of macaroni. Repeat the layers, cover the last layer of macaroni thickly with sauce, sprinkle the surface lightly with bread crumbs or extra grated cheese and add a few small pieces of butter. Bake in a hot oven (220 °C, 425 °F) for about 20 min.

Cut the rind off the bacon slices, roll each one up and place in a baking pan with the cut ends underneath. Bake under the macaroni dish for 10-15 min., until the bacon rolls are crisp. Use as a garnish, or serve separately.

6 - 7 servings

GRILLED LIVER SNACKS

Use lamb or chicken livers. Cut into neat pieces about 1-in. across, making sure no tubes are left in them, and that they are free of fat and gristle. Mix salt and freshly ground black pepper in a plastic bag with enough flour to coat the liver pieces. Add a pinch of paprika or cayenne pepper if you wish. Toss the liver pieces in the flour in the bag. Lift out; shake off excess flour. Grill or broil the pieces briefly, turning them once. A minute or 2 should be long enough, as they should still be slightly pink inside when done.

GRILLED BACON ROLLS

Cut the rind off thin slices, roll up each 1, and fasten with a wooden cocktail stick. Gril or broil the rolls on all sides, turning them often. Remove the sticks (which will be charred) before serving.

ONION RINGS FOR A MIXED GRILL

Peel and slice small or medium-sized onions, and separate the rings. Dry well in a paper towel. Heat deep fat until hazing, and fry the onion rings until soft and turning brown. Drain over the pan on a perforated spoon, and then on kitchen paper.

FRIED BREAD FOR A MIXED GRILL

Small squares of bread without crusts can be deep-fried. They must be turned once in the hot fat, and drained as soon as they are slightly brown. They burn easily.

Alternatively, they can be shallow-fried, like croutes. Make sure the first side is crisp before turning; otherwise the bread will stay soggy.

MIXED GRILL

Use the recipes for baked Cocktail Sausages, Grilled Liver Snacks, Grilled Bacon Rolls, Onion Rings, and Fried Bread above. Add the recipes for Grilled Kidneys and Grilled Mushrooms from elsewhere in this book, and also the recipes for Fried Eggs and Grilled Lamb Cutlets if you like.

Cook all your chosen ingredients, beginning with those that will take longest (usually cutlets). Fry eggs and grill liver snacks and mushrooms last. Keep them hot until required. Sprinkle with chopped parsley and a few drops of melted butter and lemon juice just before serving, if you are not serving a sauce.

APPLE LOAF

4 cups flour, sifted	1 cooking apple, peeled, cored, and sliced
Pinch of salt	
1 tsp. baking powder	Milk to mix
½ cup butter	1 cup confectioners' sugar sifted
½ cup lard	
2 eggs, beaten	A little water
⅓ cup currants	1 tart eating apple (red), cored, and sliced
⅓ cup raisins, seeded	

Dip the fruit in a little lemon juice as soon as prepared, to prevent discoloration.

Sift together the flour, salt, and baking powder. Rub in the fat, mix in the beaten egg, currants, raisins, cooking apple, and milk. Mix well. Turn into a 1-lb. lined loaf pan and bake in a moderate oven at 190 °C, 375 °F, for 40-45 min., or until springy and browned. When cool, spread the loaf with a thin icing made with confectioners' sugar and water, and decorate with sliced eating apple. Serve for tea, or brunch.

6- 8 servings

TRIFLE (TRADITIONAL)

4 individual sponge cakes	¼ cup almonds (blanched and shredded)
Raspberry *or* strawberry jam	1¼ cup Custard using 1¼ cup milk, 1 egg and 1 egg yolk
6 macaroons (12 miniature macaroons)	⅝ cup heavy cream
⅝ cup sherry	1 egg white
Grated rind of ½ lemon	2-4 tbs. sugar

Decoration:

Glacé cherries	Angelica

Split the sponge cakes into 2 and spread the lower halves with jam. Replace tops. Arrange in a glass dish and cover with macaroons and miniatures. Soak with sherry, and sprinkle with lemon rind and almonds. Cover with the custard and leave to cool. Beat the cream, egg white, and sugar together until stiff and pile on top of the trifle. Decorate with glacé cherries and angelica.

Fruit trifles, such as apricot or gooseberry, are made by substituting layers of pureed or chopped fruit for the jam.

6 servings

BRANDY SNAPS

5 tbs. sugar	4 tbs. flour
2 tbs. butter *or*	1 level tsp.
margarine	ground ginger
1 tbs. corn syrup	

Cream sugar, fat, and syrup, and stir in the sifted flour and ginger. Make into 12-16 small balls and place well apart on greased baking sheets — these cookies spread. Bake in a cool oven (150 °C, 300 °F) until a rich brown color. Allow to cool slightly, remove from sheet with a knife, and, while soft enough, roll around the handle of a wooden spoon; remove when set. The snaps may be filled with sweetened and flavored cream.

12- 16 Brandy Snaps
Cooking time – 10- 15 min.

FRUIT PUNCH

2 lb. large	1 large can
fleshy cooking	of pears (only
apples	a little fruit
¾ cup sugar	is required)
5 cups water	A few cherries
2 lemons	5 cups ginger
	beer *or* cider

Peel and core the apples and cut up small. Simmer with the sugar, water, and rind of the lemons for 15 min. in a covered saucepan. Strain through muslin and allow the liquid to cool. Add to this the liquid from the pears and the juice of the lemons. Stone a few cherries, spear on cocktail sticks, and put them in the glasses. Dice a little of the pears and put a few pieces in each glass together with some thinly peeled pieces of lemon rind, if liked. Add the ginger beer or cider to the pear and apple juice mixture and serve in the glasses.

Informal Parties

An informal party can be planned or "just happen," and it may or may not have a theme. Food can be served on a buffet, or on small tables from which people help themselves. It may be any kind of fare, depending on the time of day or night, the weather, and the party's theme, if it has one; but it usually consists of finger or fork food, or other easy-to-eat dishes.

Wine and cheese, beer and sausage, and pancake parties are all informal parties with a theme.

For a wine and cheese party, serve either a selection of cheeses from one country, or just one or two really big pieces of cheese; they look more dramatic than small wedges. Decorate cheeses with various fresh fruits in contrasting colors, and offer crisp lettuce leaves and raw celery sticks in mugs instead of more formal salads. Serve homemade breads from other sections of this book with the cheeses, and follow with ice creams and really hot coffee.

For a beer and sausage party, serve a selection of salami and other cooked sausages and cold cuts which you can buy ready to serve. Add any sausage recipes from other sections of this book and the salads and ices suggested for a Pancake Party.

PANCAKE PARTIES

A Pancake Party is good value at any time of year. It is more unusual than a Wine and Cheese Party or a Beer and Sausage Party, so a selection of recipes is given below.

For any Pancake Party, make up a good quantity of batter — enough to give each person three or four pancakes. Fry the pancakes shortly before the guests arrive. Stack them flat, one on top of another, with wax paper between them. They reheat quickly and easily if covered with foil and placed in a very cool oven.

Most fillings can also be made ahead and reheated. Make 3 or 4 kinds and keep them warm, or reheat them in a bain-marie or double boiler.

The usual way to serve pancakes is on a side table or buffet. Each guest is given a plate, a pancake, and the filling of his choice, from the selection standing either in a bain-marie or on an electric hot plate. Salads and ices are refreshing with the main savory and sweet pancakes.

For all informal parties like this, be sure that plenty of paper napkins are at hand to save greasy fingers-and furniture.

71

PANCAKE BATTER

1 cup sifted	1¼ cups milk
flour	Salt-pinch
1 egg	

Mix the flour, egg, milk, and salt into a smooth batter; let it stand for ½ hr.

To fry, use a small, clean frying pan. Add a small amount of cooking oil or rub pan with pork or bacon rind and heat until the fat just begins to smoke or until a few drops of water bounce and sputter when dropped on the frying pan. Tip in enough batter to coat the bottom of the pan, and swirl the pan to make it do so. Fry until the pancake is set underneath. Lift with a spatula and turn over. Fry the second side very briefly. Keep warm on wax paper until all the pancakes are fried.

SAVORY PANCAKES WITH BACON

| Pancake batter | Drippings |
| 4 bacon strips | |

While the batter is standing for ½ hr., remove the rind from the bacon, cut the bacon into small pieces, and fry gently. Remove from frying pan, draining off the fat, and stir into the batter. Put a little drippings into the frying pan and heat until smoking hot. Quickly pour in enough batter to coat the bottom of the pan evenly. Cook until brown underneath, turn, and brown on the other side. Serve immediately with broiled or grilled mushrooms.

4 servings

SAVORY PANCAKES WITH CHEESE

1 small onion	1 tbs. milk
4 oz. cheese	Salt and pepper
2 tbs. butter *or*	Pancake batter
margarine	

Grate the onion and cheese. Put into a saucepan, add the butter or margarine, and stir in the milk. Season to taste. Heat gently until thoroughly hot.

Make the pancakes, spread with the hot filling, and roll up. Serve immediately.

4 servings

PANCAKES STUFFED WITH KIDNEYS IN PORT WINE

4 kidneys	1 tbs. port
1 small onion	Salt and pepper
or 2 shallots	1¼ cups Tomato
2 tbs. butter *or*	Sauce
margarine	Watercress to
⅝ cup Basic	garnish
Brown Sauce	Pancake Batter

Skin the kidneys and remove the cores. Soak for 5 min. in cold water. Dry, and cut into ¼-in. slices. Chop the onion or shallots finely. Heat the fat in a sauté pan, and fry them slightly. Then put in the sliced kidney and shake and toss over the heat for about 5 min. Drain off the surplus fat and add the brown sauce, port, salt, and pepper. Stir over a gentle heat until really hot, but do not let the mixture boil.

Make the pancakes. Spread with hot filling, and roll up. Serve immediately, garnished with watercress, and with Tomato Sauce in a separate sauce boat.

4 servings

SAVORY PANCAKES WITH TUNA AND SHRIMPS

1 large green	½-⅝ cup
pepper	commercial
2 tbs. butter	sour cream
¼ cup flour	3 tbs. light
1 7-oz. can tuna	table cream
fish, flaked	Pancake Batter
¾ cup shrimps,	
peeled	
Salt and pepper	

Remove the stalk and seeds from the pepper. Cut into ¼-in. pieces, and blanch in boiling salted water for 1 min. Drain. Melt the butter, add the flour, and cook over moderate heat for 2 min. Blend in the flaked tuna, the shrimps, blanched pepper, and the sour and light table cream. Stir over gentle heat until hot but not boiling. Season to taste, and keep warm.

Make the pancakes. Heat a little drippings in a frying pan, pour in enough batter to coat the bottom, and shake. Cook until brown, turn, and brown the second side. Spread the pancakes with the filling, roll or fold them, and serve while hot.

4 servings

GRILLED MUSHROOMS

12 mushrooms	Buttered toast
Salt and pepper	Chopped parsley
Butter *or* bacon	Lemon juice
fat	

Wash, peel, and trim the stalks. Season and brush with melted butter *or* bacon fat. Cook under a hot grill or broiler, turning them once. Serve in a hot dish or on rounds of buttered toast, with a sprinkling of chopped parsley and a squeeze of lemon juice. A pinch of very finely chopped marjoram, sprinkled on each mushroom prior to grilling, imparts an excellent flavor.

6 servings

BAKED TOMATOES

6 tomatoes	Finely chopped
A little butter	tarragon
or margarine	(optional)
Salt and pepper	Brown bread
Sugar	crumbs (optional)

Wash the tomatoes and cut them in halves. Put them in a greased, deep baking dish. Season and sprinkle each with a pinch of sugar and a pinch of chopped tarragon, if used. Put a tiny piece of butter on each or cover with foil Bake in a moderate oven (180 °C, 350 °F) until soft — about 20 min.

Alternatively, cut the tomatoes in half horizontally or make crosswise cuts in the top of each. Press the cut portion into browned bread crumbs before baking, and top with the butter or margarine.

6 servings

RICE SALAD

½ cup rice	Small red *or*
1-2 tbs. olive	green pepper
oil	(capsicum)
1-2 tbs.	2-3 gherkins
vinegar	Seasoning
¼ cup cooked	1 tsp. chopped
peas	chives *or* onion
¼ cup cooked	Watercress
diced carrots	

Cook the rice in boiling salted water, drain, and mix with the oil and vinegar

while still hot. The smaller quantity of oil and vinegar gives a fairly dry salad. Add the peas, carrots, finely chopped uncooked red or green pepper, chopped gherkins, seasoning, and chives or onion. Put into a dish and garnish with watercress.

5- 6 servings
Cooking time – 12 min. (approx.)

ORANGE SALAD

4 sweet oranges	Chopped
½ tsp. sugar	tarragon and
1 tbs. French	chervil *or*
dressing	chopped mint

Peel the oranges with a saw-edged knife, so that all pith is removed. Cut out the natural orange sections. Place in a salad bowl; sprinkle with sugar. Pour the dressing over and sprinkle with tarragon and chervil, or with chopped mint.

4- 6 servings

CARROT SALAD

3 large carrots	Finely chopped
6 lettuce leaves	parsley
French Dressing	

Grate the carrots finely and serve on a bed of lettuce leaves. Sprinkle with the French Dressing. Garnish with chopped parsley. Grated, raw carrot can be used with success in many salads. It should be grated very finely to be digestible and sprinkled with lemon juice or French Dressing as soon as grated to retain its bright color.

6 servings

COOKED CAULIFLOWER SALAD

1 large cauliflower	Vinaigrette Sauce

Stream the cauliflower then divide carefully into flowerets. Arrange the flowerets neatly in a salad bowl and pour the sauce over while the cauliflower is still warm. Serve when quite cold.

6 servings

Savory Pancakes with Shrimps

Lardy Cake

POTATO SALAD

6 large new potatoes *or* waxy old potatoes	1 tsp. chopped mint
	1 tsp. chopped chives *or* spring onion
French Dressing *or* Vinaigrette Sauce	Salt and pepper
2 heaping tbs. chopped parsley	

Cook the potatoes in their skins until just soft. Peel and dice while still hot. Mix while hot with the dressing and the herbs and a little seasoning. Serve cold.

6 servings

TOMATO SALAD

6 large firm tomatoes	French Dressing *or* cream salad dressing
Salt and pepper	Finely chopped parsley

Skin and slice the tomatoes. Season lightly. Pour the dressing over the tomatoes. Sprinkle with chopped parsley.

6 servings

SWEET PANCAKES

1 cup flour	1¼ cups milk
1 egg	Pinch salt

Apple Pancakes

Confectioners' sugar 1 lemon	A little cooking fat

Put about ½ tbs. of cooking fat into a clean frying pan and heat until it is just beginning to smoke. Quickly pour in enough batter to coat thinly the bottom of the pan, tilting the pan to make sure the batter runs over evenly. Move the frying pan over a quick heat until the pancake is set and browned underneath. Make sure the pancake is loose at the sides, then toss, or turn with a spatula. Brown on the other side and turn onto a sugared paper. Sprinkle with confectioners' sugar and lemon juice, roll up, and keep hot while cooking the rest. Serve dredged with confectioners' sugar and pieces of cut lemon.

Other flavorings, such as apple, jam, orange, tangerine, or brandy may be used, as follows:

Apple Pancakes Add grated lemon rind to the batter. Fill with Apple Sauce mixed with seedless raisins and a little lemon juice.

Jam Pancakes Spread with jam before rolling up. Cherry jam is good, topped with whipped cream.

Orange Pancakes Make the pancakes, sprinkle with orange juice, and serve with pieces of cut orange.

Tangerine Pancakes Add grated tangerine rind to the batter. Sprinkle with tangerine juice before rolling up.

Brandy filling for pancakes Cream together ¼ cup butter and 2 tbs. sugar until soft. Work in 1 tbs. brandy and 1 tsp. lemon juice. Spread the pancakes with this mixture. Roll up and put immediately into the serving dish.

SYRUP FOR WATER ICES

2 lb. sugar	2½ cups water

Place the sugar and water in a strong saucepan. Allow the sugar to dissolve over low heat. Do not stir. When the sugar has dissolved, gently boil the mixture for 10 min., or if a candy thermometer is available, until it registers about 100 °C, 212 °F. Remove scum as it rises. Strain, cool, and store.

2½ cups syrup

LEMON WATER ICE

| 6 lemons | 3¾ cups syrup, |
| 2 oranges | as above |

Peel the fruit and place the rind in a basin. Add the hot syrup, cover, and cool. Add the juice of the lemons and oranges. Strain, chill, and freeze.

6 servings

LEMON OR ORANGE SHERBET

2½ cups water	1¼ cups lemon *or*
1 cup sugar	orange juice
2 egg whites	

Dissolve the sugar in the water. Boil for 10 min., strain, and cool. Add the juice and stiffly whisked egg whites. Freeze and serve at once.

6 servings

ALFRESCO PARTIES

An alfresco party takes place outdoors, and guests help themselves to food and drinks when they like, either from a long buffet table or smaller ones. An alfresco party can take place at any time of day — even at breakfast-time — or in the evening. Once the food is prepared, the hostess' only care is to see that any hot dishes are kept really hot and that all the dishes are replenished when required. Dishes that are almost empty look rather forlorn.

SANDWICHES

The term "sandwich" has a much wider meaning today than when it was first introduced by the Earl of Sandwich and applied only to slices of meat placed between bread and butter. We have now "open" or continental sandwiches, club or two-decker sandwiches, toasted sandwiches, and attractively shaped party sandwiches. Their fillings are now immensely varied, savory or sweet, minced, or shredded and mixed with various butters, sauces, and seasonings. Making sandwiches requires little skill, just plenty of imagination and an eye for color.

The bread for sandwiches should be fresh but not too new; French rolls, Vienna rolls, whole wheat, or milk bread make an interesting change from ordinary loaves. Creamed butter is more easily spread than ordinary butter. When ordinary butter is used, it should first be beaten to a cream (add 1 tsp. hot water to ½ lb. butter) to make spreading easier. Savory butters give piquancy and variety to other fillings and can be used alone for rolled sandwiches.

Sandwiches simplify entertaining, for they can be prepared well in advance and can be served buffet style, leaving the hostess free to mix with her guests. If prepared some time before required, sandwiches keep fresh and moist if wrapped in greaseproof paper and then in a damp cloth, or if put into a plastic bag, or wrapped in waxed paper or aluminum foil, and kept in the refrigerator or a cool place. Sandwiches with different fillings should be wrapped separately to prevent the flavors mixing.

SANDWICH FILLINGS

Savory Fillings:

1) Anchovies mixed with hard-boiled egg yolk, cheese, and butter, with a sprinkling of cayenne. Spread the bread with curry butter.

2) Canned tuna fish mixed with salad cream and chopped parsley, with a dash of cayenne.

3) Canned salmon, mashed with lemon juice and chopped chives, spread on a bed of cucumber slices.

4) Minced, cooked, smoked haddock, seasoned and mixed to a smooth paste with butter and anchovy paste.

5) Very thin slices of cooked chicken and ham, seasoned and placed between bread spread with curry butter.

6) Very finely shredded celery, moistened slightly with heavy cream, seasoned to taste.

7) Finely grated cheese mixed to a smooth paste with a little seasoning, anchovy paste, and butter.

8) A layer of finely chopped gherkin, olives, and capers, mixed with mayonnaise sauce, and covered with a layer of creamed cheese.

9) Mashed sardines, a little lemon juice and seasoning, mixed to a smooth paste with butter.

10) Sardines mashed with an equal amount of grated cheese until smooth, seasoned to taste, with a little lemon juice or vinegar added, and sufficient cream or milk to moisten.

11) Minced cooked chicken and ham or tongue combined with creamed cheese and egg yolk, seasoned and moistened with oil.

12) Finely shredded lettuce and watercress seasoned with salt and mixed with mayonnaise.

13) Thin slices of Gruyère cheese on slices of bread and butter, spread with French mustard seasoned with pepper.

14) Slices of hard-boiled egg, seasoned, covered with watercress or mustard and cress, sprinkled with equal quantities of oil and vinegar.

15) Canned pâté de foie gras.

16) Minced cooked chicken and ham or tongue moistened with a little liquid butter and mayonnaise.

17) Lightly spread caviar sprinkled with lemon juice and a little cayenne. The bread may be spread with shrimp butter.

Sweet Fillings:

1) Bananas mashed with lemon juice and ground almonds and sprinkled with sugar.

2) A layer of creamed cheese or cottage cheese covered with a layer of fresh strawberries or raspberries sprinkled with sugar.

3) Softened creamed cheese mixed with canned crushed pineapple and finely chopped preserved ginger.

4) Chocolate spread mixed with chopped walnuts and cottage cheese.

5) Chopped pears, dates, and walnuts mixed with golden syrup.

6) Thick slices of banana sprinkled with coarsely grated chocolate.

OPEN SANDWICHES

Use ¼-in.-thick slices of white or brown bread. Spread with softened butter and any of the party sandwich fillings below. Garnish with stuffed olives, slices of hard-boiled egg, small pieces of tomato, watercress, cream cheese, etc.

The appeal of these sandwiches lies in the artistic way in which the garnish is arranged. They must look colorful, fresh, and tempting. Remember that garnishes stay fresher if arranged vertically and if kept under a damp cloth until serving time.

SAVORY SCANDINAVIAN GARNISHES

1) Samsoe cheese with radish.

2) Tongue with Russian salad, cucumber, and a twist of tomato.

Cold Table with Open Sandwiches

them, and cook in the water or stock until soft. Then lift them out to be used in salad. Cool the stock; add the other vegetables and spices. Beat the egg white and add to the stock. Bring slowly to simmering point and simmer very gently for 1 hr. Strain through a linen cloth. Season and reheat. This soup can be served hot or cold. If cold, 1½ tbs. gelatin should be dissolved in a little stock and added to the whole before cooling.

6 servings

ROLLMOP HERRINGS

These make a most economical hors d'oeuvre by themselves and add flavor to a mixed hors d'oeuvres.

6 large herrings	4-6 small
¼ cup salt	gherkins
2½ cups water	Chilies
2½ cups malt	1 tbs. pickling
vinegar	spice
2 large onions	
2 bay leaves	

Clean, bone, and filet the herrings. Mix the salt and water together and put the herrings to soak in this for 2 hr. Lift out of the brine, drain, and put into a shallow dish, covering with the vinegar and leaving for several hours. Shred the onions finely. Drain the herring filets, reserving the vinegar, put 1 tbs. of onion onto each filet and roll firmly. Secure with small wooden cocktail sticks if possible. Put into jars with bay leaves, gherkins, and chilies (use 1 per jar). Pour the vinegar from the dish into a saucepan and boil for a few minutes with the pickling spice. Cool and strain over the herrings. Cover the jars and store in a cool place. They will keep for 2-3 weeks prepared this way. Note that the herrings are not cooked for this dish.

6-12 servings – or filets can be divided into halves for part of a mixed hors d'oeuvres

3) Egg and crisply fried bacon, with cucumber and a twist of tomato.

4) Liver pâté with mushrooms sautéed in butter, shreds of crisply fried bacon, tomato, lettuce, and gherkins.

5) Luncheon meat with horseradish cream and an orange butterfly.

6) Danish blue cheese with black grapes.

7) Salami (without garlic) with raw onion rings and chopped parsley.

8) Luncheon meat with young carrots, peas in mayonnaise, and cucumber.

9) Danish blue cheese with chopped apple coated with French Dressing, topped with a parsley sprig.

CONSOMMÉ ROSÉ

4 raw beets	1 onion
Sugar	1 bay leaf
5 cups vegetable	1 clove garlic
water *or* stock	1 clove
3 carrots	1 egg white
1 stick of	Salt and pepper
celery	
1½ lb. tomatoes	
or 1 large can	
tomatoes	

Scrub and peel the beets, slice and sugar

CUCUMBER AND SEAFOOD ROLLS

1 large thin *or*	Mayonnaise
2 small thin	1 2-oz. can
cucumbers	anchovy filets
Oil	Stuffed olives
Vinegar	Parsley

Seasoning
⅝ cup crab *or*
  lobster meat

Peel the cucumbers and cut them into 1-in. thick slices. Cut out the center portion, place rings on a dish, and pour over a little oil and vinegar. Season well. Pound the crab or lobster meat or blend in an electric blender. Mix the meat with mayonnaise. Drain the cucumber shapes and fill each cavity with this mixture. Twist a whole anchovy filet around each and place a slice of stuffed olive on top. Garnish with parsley.

About 10 rolls

LIVER PÂTÉ

1 lb. calf *or* pig *or* poultry liver	A few gherkins (optional)
4 oz. very lean ham *or* bacon	1-2 hard-boiled eggs (optional)
1 small onion	A little cream (optional)
6 tbs. butter	Extra butter
Seasoning	
Pinch of mixed herbs	

Liver Pâté

Cut the liver, ham, and onion into small pieces. Heat the butter in a pan and cook the liver, ham, and onion for about 6 min. — no longer. Put through a very fine mincer twice to give a very smooth mixture. Add the seasoning, herbs, and chopped gherkins and chopped hard-boiled eggs, too, if wished. For a very soft pâté also add a little cream. Put into a dish and cook for about ½ hr. in a moderate oven (170 °C, 350 °F) covered, and standing in a dish of cold water to prevent the mixture becoming dry. When the pâté is cooked, cover with a layer of melted butter. Serve cut in slices on a bed of crisp lettuce and accompanied with hot toast and butter.

4- 6 servings

MAKING COLD MOUSSES

A cold savory mousse makes an excellent first course. It may be made with a custard base alone or have cream added. If it contains cream, avoid a creamy main course. A mousse or soufflé may be made in one big mold or in individual ones. In general, mousses are made with pounded or pureed cooked fish, meat, or vegetables, usually mixed with a starchy substance or panada, and a liquid thickened with egg yolks, and sometimes with gelatin. The stiffly beaten egg whites can then be added, and the mixture poured into the carefully prepared mold or molds to set.

HAM MOUSSE

½ lb. cooked ham	1 drop red food coloring
Salt and pepper	1 cup cream *or* milk
Grated nutmeg	
1¼ cups rich brown stock *or* consommé	1 tbs. chopped mushroom
1 tbs. gelatin	¼ cup firm Aspic Jelly
⅝ cup Aspic Jelly	
2 tbs. white stock	

Tie a band of stiff paper around a china soufflé dish about 5-in. diameter so that it stands about 2-in. higher than the dish.

Pass the ham twice through the mincer, and sieve it; or blend in an electric blender. Season with salt, pepper, and nutmeg. Add the brown stock or consommé which should be well-colored and flavored with a little tomato paste or puree. Dissolve the gelatin in the aspic, together with the white stock. Color with red food coloring, and add to the ham. Whip the cream lightly; fold it into the mixture. When it is just beginning to set, pour it into the prepared soufflé dish. Allow to set. Add the chopped mushroom to the firm aspic, cold but liquid, and pour over the top of the mold. When set, remove the paper. Serve with green salad.

VOL-AU-VENTS AND PATTIES

Vol-au-Vent or patty shells filled with savory mixtures can be served hot or cold. If a mixture is being put into cold pastry shells, make sure it is quite cold. If, on the other hand, it is being put into hot shells, heat the filling and the pastry separately, and put together at the last minute, so that the filling does not make the pastry soft. Vol-au-Vent shells can be bought uncooked, frozen, or ready to use. They can also, of course, be made at home, using frozen or homemade Puff Pastry.

To Make a Vol-au-Vent Shell

Roll out the Puff Pastry to about ¾ in. thickness, and, with a cutter previously dipped in flour, cut into a round or oval shape, as desired. Cut cleanly, without dragging or twisting the pastry. Place on a baking sheet; brush over the top of the pastry with beaten egg. With a smaller, floured cutter cut an inner ring, cutting the pastry to about ½ its depth. Bak in a very hot oven (230 °C, 450 °F). When baked, remove the lid and scoop out the soft inside.

To Make Patty Shells

Roll out the puff or flaky pastry to a thickness of ⅛ in. and cut into rounds with a 2½- or 3-in. cutter. Remove the centers from half of these rounds with a 1¼- or 1½ in. cutter. Turn the pastry upside down after cutting. Moisten the plain halves and place the ringed halves evenly on top. Prick the centers. Place on a baking tray and allow to stand for at least 10 min. in a cold place. Glaze the ringed halves and the small lids and bake in a very hot oven (230 °C, 450 °F). When baked, remove and scoop out any soft inside part. If liked, the shells can be made as vol-au-vent shells (above), using smaller cutters.

SUGGESTED FILLINGS FOR VOL-AU-VENTS AND PATTY SHELLS

Quantities given are enough to fill 12 medium-sized vol-au-vent shells or about 16 cone-shaped shells (allowing a liberal amount of filling).

Chicken

1¼ cups thick sauce made with ½ milk and ½ chicken stock	2-3 cups diced cooked chicken (approx.) Seasoning

Mix together well, and if possible add just 1 tbs. cream.

Mushroom

¾ lb. mushrooms ¼ cup butter or margarine 1½ cups milk	⅜ cup flour Seasoning Cayenne pepper

Chop the mushrooms into small pieces and toss in the hot butter for a few min. Add 1¼ cups of milk and cook gently for about 10 min. Blend the flour with the other ¼ cup milk; add to the mushroom mixture. Season well and boil until smooth and thick. Stir as the mixture cools. If wished, add 1 tbs. heavy cream. Dust with cayenne pepper when the shells are filled.

Sausage and Apple Filling

2 medium onions, peeled and chopped 1 lb. sausage meat 2 apples, peeled, cored, and chopped	1 tbs. chopped parsley 2 tsp. mixed herbs Salt and pepper 1 beaten egg Melted butter

Sauté the onions in the butter for 4-5 min. Add sausage meat, apples, parsley, herbs and seasoning, and fry 3 min. more. Cool slightly, and add the beaten egg. Pile on toasted bread or in vol-au-vent or patty shells and bake in a moderate oven (350 °F) for 10-15 min. or until just set. Top with toasted bread or a pastry "hat," if appropriate.

4 savories

Sardine

1 small can	2 tsp. grated
of sardines	Parmesan cheese
1 tbs. White *or*	*or* 1 tbs. grated
Tomato Sauce	cheddar cheese
Salt and pepper	
Few drops of	
lemon juice	

Remove the bones and mash the sardines. Mix with the white or tomato sauce (if using white sauce, add a few drops of anchovy flavoring). Season; blend with a few drops of lemon juice and the cheese.

"ANGELS ON HORSEBACK"

12 oysters	½ tsp. chopped
12 small thin	parsley
slices of bacon	Lemon juice
Paprika *or*	12 small rounds
cayenne pepper	of fried bread
½ tsp. chopped	*or* 4 slices of
shallot *or* onion	toast

Remove the gills of the oysters; trim the bacon, cutting each piece just large enough to roll around an oyster; season with paprika or cayenne pepper and sprinkle on a little shallot and parsley. Lay an oyster on each, add a few drops of lemon juice, roll up tightly, and secure the bacon in position with a fine skewer. Cook in a frying pan, under the grill, or in a hot oven (220 °C, 425 °F) *just long enough* to crisp the bacon (further cooking would harden the oysters). Remove the skewers, and serve on the croutes.

4 servings or 12 small savories
Cooking time – 5- 10 min.

"CREAM" CHEESE FLAN

Shortcrust Pastry,	2 tsp. sugar
frozen *or* using	½ cup creamed
1½ cups flour,	cheese
etc., if home-	¼ tsp. grated
made	lemon rind
½ tbs. gelatin	1 tbs. lemon
2 tbs. water	juice

¼ cup milk	⅝ cup cream
1 egg yolk	

Line an 8-in. flan ring with the pastry. Prick with a fork and bake in a preheated oven (450 °F) for about 12 min. or until lightly browned. Soak the gelatin in the water for 2-3 min. Heat the milk and dissolve the gelatin in it. Beat together the egg yolk and sugar and add the hot milk. Combine with the cheese; stir in the lemon rind and juice. Cool. Whip the cream and fold into cheese mixture. Pour into baked flan shell; chill for 2 hr.

HALIBUT WITH ORANGE AND WATERCRESS SALAD

4 5-6 oz. pieces	Mayonnaise
halibut	1 bunch
Seasoning	watercress
1 head lettuce	(¼ lb.)
	2 small oranges

Prepare the filets, season, fold in half, and steam for 10-15 min.; allow to cool. Shred the outer leaves of lettuce and arrange on a salad dish. Place the cooked filets on this and coat them evenly with mayonnaise. Garnish with the remaining lettuce, fairly large sprigs of watercress, and slices of orange.

Note: Turbot may be substituted for halibut.

4 servings

BRAISED BEEF IN ASPIC

1½ lb. filet	French mustard
of beef,	3 cups Aspic
previously	Jelly
braised	Cooked peas
1 jar of meat	Cooked carrots
paste	

Braise the beef the previous day, if possible, and allow it to become quite cold. Trim into an oblong shape and cut lengthwise into slices. Spread each slice alternately with meat paste and mustard; put the slices together again and press between 2 boards. Set a layer of Aspic Jelly at the bottom of a cake or bread pan and dec-

Angels on Horseback with sausage "Spiral" Rolls and Cocktail Sausages

Halibut with Orange and Watercress

orate with cooked peas and rings of cooked carrots. Pour on another layer of cold, liquid Aspic Jelly and allow it to set. Place the prepared beef on top, fill the mold with Aspic Jelly, and allow to set. Unmold onto an oval dish and decorate with chopped aspic. Serve with an appropriate salad or rice.

6 servings

COLD CHICKEN, GARNISHED

1 cold boiled chicken *or* fowl *or* 8 drumsticks	2½ cups Béchamel *or* Supreme Sauce
4 tbs. gelatin	1¼ cups Aspic Jelly
	6 tbs. bottled salad cream

Garnish — selection of

Cucumber slices	Olive
Pimiento, red, cut in fancy shapes	Lemon rind Green leek
Mushroom	

Cut up the chicken if required. Skin and trim the parts, then chill them. Dissolve gelatin in a little hot water; stir into the warm sauce. Add the salad cream. Tammy the sauce (i.e. pass it through a thick cloth) to get a smooth, glossy result. When cool enough to be a good coating consistency, coat the chicken. Decorate with the chosen garnish, and allow to set. Coat with cold liquid Aspic Jelly of a coating consistency, pouring it carefully over each piece with a tablespoon. Serve with a good salad.

A cold chicken can also be attractively garnished simply with a coating of semi-liquid Aspic Jelly and topped with fruits such as green grapes, apricots, or cherries, with tiny pieces of tomato or red pepper and walnuts or almonds.

6 servings

MIXED-VEGETABLE SUMMER SALAD

3 large new potatoes	1 tbs. chopped parsley
3 new turnips	1 tsp. chopped mint
1¼ cups shelled peas	Salad dressing
½ bunch new carrots	

Cook the vegetables and slice the carrots, potatoes, and young turnips. Save some of each vegetable for garnish, and toss the rest in the salad dressing with the herbs. Put the mixture in a suitable dish and garnish with the remainder. Baste with a little French Dressing.

MIXED-VEGETABLE WINTER SALAD

1 cauliflower	Salad dressing
2 large carrots	Watercress *or*
1 parsnip *or* 2 turnips	fine cress
1 cooked beet	A little French Dressing
1 small can of peas	

Steam the cauliflower, carrots, and parsnip or turnips. Divide the cauliflower into flowerets. Dice the carrots, parsnip or turnips, and beet, or cut into neat rounds with a cutter. Rinse and drain the peas. Mix all trimmings and uneven pieces of vegetable lightly with salad dressing — include some of the peas. Put this mixture into a dish, preferably oblong in shape. Cover with lines of each vegetable, very neatly arranged and with suitable colors adjoining. Garnish the edges with watercress or fine cress. Baste the surface with French Dressing.

For Russian Salad, mix the prepared vegetables with mayonnaise instead of salad dressing.

4- 6 servings

Cold Chicken garnished with Pimiento Flowers

KNICKERBOCKER GLORY

2½ cups red jelly	2½ cups Melba Sauce
2½ cups yellow jelly	⅓ cup chopped walnuts
1 small can chopped peaches	⅝ cup sweetened whipped cream
1 small can pineapple	8 maraschino cherries
1 qt. Vanilla Ice Cream	

Make the jellies, allow to set, then whip with a fork. Place small portions of chopped fruit in the bottom of tall sundae glasses. Cover these with 1 tbs. of whipped jelly. Place a scoop or slice of ice cream on top of the jelly. Coat the ice cream with Melba Sauce. Repeat again with fruit, jelly, ice cream, and sauce. Sprinkle with chopped nuts. Top with sweetened whipped cream. Place a cherry on top of each

6 individual glasses

STRAWBERRY CREAM BUNS

**Chou Pastry using 1 cup flour, etc.
Confectioners' sugar**

83

Filling:

1¼ cups sweetened heavy or whipping cream flavored with vanilla extract *or*
1¼ cups Confectioners' Custard

Pipe out and bake the buns like Chocolate Profiteroles. Split them, remove any damp parts inside, and dry out. When cold, fill the shells with the cream or custard, with the strawberries embedded in it. Replace the lids, and dust with confectioners' sugar.

CONFECTIONERS' CUSTARD

1¼ cups milk	2 tbs. sugar
3 tbs. cornstarch	½ tsp. vanilla
2 yolks *or*	extract
1 whole egg	

Blend the cornstarch with the milk, stir in the egg yolks and sugar, and cook over low heat until thick. Beat in the vanilla. Allow to cool.

BARBECUES

At a barbecue, guests may grill their own meat on the prepared fire, and season or dress it themselves. Steaks, chops, sausages, and spareribs are the most usual mixed grills served; they are placed on trays, usually on a trestle or similar table not too near the fire. Other things to serve are salt, pepper, pots of mustard, crisp lettuce, tomatoes, homemade breads, butter, and fresh fruit.

The success of a barbecue depends on the weather. Rain can make cooking impossible. If there is a risk of rain, it is wise to have 1 or 2 dishes consisting of "grills," such as ham steaks, and ready-prepared additions such as rice, which can be assembled quickly indoors to make a substantial main course.

HAM STEAKS WITH RICE

1¼ cups rice	2 eating apples,
2 tbs. chopped	cored and
parsley	chopped
Seasoning	1½ cups grated
¼ cup butter	cheese
2 cups white	4 thick ham
bread crumbs	steaks
	Parsley

Cook the rice in boiling salted water until tender. Drain, stir in the chopped parsley and seasoning, and keep warm. Grill the ham steaks, turning them once. While they grill, sauté the bread crumbs in butter, add the diced apple, and cook for 2-3 min. Remove from the heat and stir in half the grated cheese.

Place rice in a serving dish; arrange the ham steaks overlapping, with apple-crumb mixture between each slice; sprinkle with grated cheese; replace under the hot broiler for a min. or 2. Garnish with parsley.

4 servings

CUMBERLAND LAMB PIES

12 oz. ground	A pinch of
lamb	thyme
Shortcrust Pastry	Salt and pepper
using 3 cups	A little good
flour, etc.	stock
1 onion	Egg *or* milk
4 oz. mushrooms	
2 tsp. chopped	
parsley	

Chop and lightly fry the onion. Line 12 small round pie pans with ½ the pastry. Mix together the ground lamb, chopped onion, chopped mushrooms, parsley, thyme, and seasoning. Divide the mixture between the pans. Add to each a little stock to moisten. Cover with lids made from the rest of the pastry. Brush with egg or milk and bake in a moderate oven (180 °C, 350 °F) for about 30-45 min.

6 servings

BASIC MILK BREAD

4 cups flour	¼ cup lard *or*
1 tsp. salt	margarine
1 tbs. yeast	1¼ cups warm
½ tsp. sugar	milk (approx.)
	1 egg (optional)

Mix the salt with the warmed flour; cream the yeast with the sugar. Rub fat into flour and mix with the yeast, milk, and egg if used, to a fairly soft, light dough. Beat until mixture is smooth and leaves the sides of the bowl clean. Allow to stand in a warm place until twice its original size. Then turn onto a floured board, knead again not too heavily but until there are only small holes in the dough, and put into the prepared pans. Let stand until the dough is well up the sides of the pan, then bake in a hot oven (220 °C, 425 °F).

3 - 4 loaves   Cooking time – 1 hr.

BRAIDED BREAD

Roll risen dough into 2 strips, each 10 in. long by 5 or 6 in. wide. Cut each strip almost to the top in 3 even-sized pieces and braid them as if braiding hair. Dampen and seal the ends neatly but firmly and place on a greased baking sheet. Allow to stand 10-15 min. Brush with beaten egg and place in a hot oven (230 °C, 450 °F). Bake 20-30 min., reducing heat after first 10 min. to 200 °C, 400 °F, or 190 °C, 375 °F.

2 loaves   Cooking time – 20 - 30 min.

WHOLE WHEAT BREAD

3½ lb. whole wheat flour	2 tbs. yeast
3½ tsp. salt	¼ cup lard
1 tsp. sugar	4⅜ cups warm water

Mix salt well with flour and warm in a large bowl. Cream the yeast with the sugar, add the warm water together with the melted fat, and mix with the flour to an elastic dough. Knead well until smooth, cover with a cloth to prevent surface evaporation, and set in a warm place to rise to double its size — about 1 hr. When the dough is sufficiently risen, it has a honeycombed appearance. The first kneading distributes the yeast and softens the gluten of the flour. Knead the dough a second time to distribute the carbonic acid gas that has formed. Continue kneading until, when the dough is cut, there are no large holes in it, but do not knead too heavily. Divide into the required number of loaves. Place in warmed greased pans, making the top round. Prick and allow to stand for 20 min. or until the dough is well up to the top of the pan. If the dough stands too long, it will collapse and give heavy bread. Bake in top middle of a very hot oven (230 °C, 450 °F) for 10-15 min., then reduce heat to fairly hot (190 °C, 375 °F), baking in all about 1 hr. When ready, the loaf should have a hollow sound when knocked on the bottom and should be well-risen and nicely browned, with a crisp crust.

4 loaves   Cooking time – 1 hr.

FANCY BREAD ROLLS (BASIC DOUGH)

2 cups flour	1 heaping tsp. sugar
1 level tsp. salt	
2 tbs. margarine	⅝ cup skim milk made from milk powder
1 tbs. fresh yeast *or* ½ tbs. dried yeast	

Sift the flour and salt into a large bowl. Leave to stand in a warm place for 10-15 min. Cut in the margarine. Mix the yeast and sugar together. Warm the milk and stir it into the yeast mixture. Make a well in the center of the flour, pour in the liquid, and mix to a soft dough. Knead for 5-10 min. on a floured surface, until the dough is smooth and glossy. Place in a greased bowl, turn over to grease the whole surface of the dough, cover with a damp cloth, and leave to rise until doubled in size. Shape as required.

Trefoils
Divide the basic dough into 8 pieces, then divide each piece into 3 bits. Form these into balls and cluster 3 together in a patty or muffin pan. Fill 8 pans, then leave in a warm place until doubled in size — about 15 min. Brush with beaten egg yolk and skim milk to glaze, and scatter on a few poppy seeds. Bake in a fairly hot oven, at 200 °C, 400 °F, for 15-20 min.

Bread Knots
Divide the dough into 8 pieces and roll each into a tube shape about 10-in. long. Tie in a loose knot. Let stand, glaze as above, place on a greased baking sheet, and bake like Trefoils.

Baby Cottage Loaves
Divide the basic dough into 8 pieces. Cut each piece into a smaller and larger piece. Shape into rounds. Place the larger rounds on a greased baking sheet, and put the smaller ones on top. Make a dip in the center of each with your finger. Let stand and glaze like Trefoils, and bake in the same way.

Strawberry Cream Buns

Mulligatawny Soup

Blue Cheese and Apple Savories

Potatoes Baked in Their Jackets

Ginger Twists
Knead 2 level tsp. ground ginger into the dough (or sift in with the flour). Divide the dough into 16 pieces and roll each out 6-in. long. Twist 2 pieces together, and place on a greased baking sheet. Let stand, glaze, and bake like Trefoils. When cooked and cool, brush over with icing made from sifted confectioners' sugar and water.

WINTER-EVENING PARTIES

Winter evening parties take place indoors, but they can be as informal as alfresco parties, especially on occasions when the guests (who include children) spend their time between the indoor warmth and the scene outside. The food is, again, served buffet style, for guests to help themselves. Any of the dishes above are suitable, or the hostess can pick ideas from other sections of this book. But she should make sure that some really heart-warming hot dishes are included, such as those that follow.

MULLIGATAWNY SOUP

1 lb. chicken	Salt
1 onion	1 carrot
1 small cooking	½ small parsnip
apple	A bunch of
2 tbs. butter *or*	herbs
margarine	Lemon juice
2 tbs. curry	¼ tsp. blackstrap
powder	molasses
¼ cup flour	1 cup boiled
5 cups bone	rice
stock *or* water	

Cut the meat in small pieces. Chop the onion and apple finely. Heat the butter in a deep pan and quickly fry the onion, then the curry powder. Add the apple and cook it gently for a few min., then stir in the flour. Add the liquid, meat, and salt, and bring slowly to simmering point, stirring all the time. Add the other vegetables, the herbs tied in muslin, and a few drops of lemon juice. Simmer until the meat is very tender, about 1 hr. Taste the soup and add more lemon juice or add blackstrap molasses to obtain a flavor that is neither predominantly sweet nor acid. Strain the soup, cut some of the meat in neat cubes, and reheat them in the soup. Boil, drain, and partly dry the rice as for curry and add it to the soup just before serving.

Note: The amount of curry powder can be varied to taste; the quantity given is for a mild flavored soup.

4- 6 servings Cooking time – from 2- 4 hr., according to the meat used

Somerset Stuffing:

1 medium-sized onion, finely chopped	2½ cups white bread crumbs
1 tbs. butter	1 tbs. raisins
6-7 oz. cooking apples	Pepper
	1 large egg, beaten

Cut through the pork chops from the outside edge to within ¾ in. of the inside edge with a sharp knife, to form a "pocket." Fry the onion in butter for 5 min. Peel, core, and grate the apples. Mix onion, bread crumbs, raisins, and pepper together. Bind with the egg. Use this mixture to stuff the "pockets" in the chops. Place in a roasting pan. Spoon over melted butter and bake in a moderately hot oven (190 °C, 375 °F) for 30 min., basting from time to time, until the chops are golden and tender. Garnish with fried onion rings.

6 servings Cooking time – 30 min.

POTATOES BAKED IN THEIR JACKETS

6 large potatoes
Butter *or* margarine *or* bacon fat

Scrub the potatoes; rinse and dry them. Brush with melted butter, or margarine, or bacon fat, or rub with a greasy butter paper. Prick with a fork. Bake on the shelves of a fairly hot oven (190 °C, 375 °F) until soft — about 1½ hr. Turn once while they are cooking. Make a cut in the top of each; insert a pat of butter or margarine. Serve in a hot vegetable dish.

New potatoes can be cooked in the same way.

6 servings

SOMERSET BAKED PORK CHOPS

6 boneless pork chops	1 large onion
2 tbs. melted butter	2 tbs. butter

PEA PUDDING

3¾ cups split peas	¼ cup butter *or* margarine
1 small onion	2 eggs
Small bunch of herbs	Salt and pepper

Soak the peas overnight; remove any discolored ones. Rinse and cover with cold, salted water. Bring slowly to boiling point in the water, to which the onion (whole) and the bunch of herbs have been added. Simmer very slowly until tender — 2-2½ hr. Drain well and rub through a sieve. Add the butter, cut in small pieces, the beaten eggs, pepper, and salt. Beat well until the ingredients are well blended. Tie tightly in a floured cloth of unbleached muslin and simmer in water for an hour. Turn out and serve very hot. Pea pudding is served with hot pickled pork and other pork and bacon dishes.

6 servings

BLUE CHEESE AND APPLE SAVORIES

3 oz. blue cheese, crumbled	Salt and pepper
2 tbs. butter *or* margarine	2-3 cooking apples
Flour for dredging	Tarragon Butter, shaped into small balls
2/3 cup bread crumbs	

Cream together the cheese and butter or margarine. Mix in the bread crumbs, using a fork. Core the apples, but do not peel them. Cut each one into 3 or 4 thick rounds. Lay them on a baking sheet or broiling tray. Season. Dredge with flour to dry, then spread each round with cheese mixture all over. Smooth the surface. Broil under high heat until the cheese bubbles and browns. Leave in a warm place until the apples slices begin to soften. Just before serving, top each slice with a small chilled ball of tarragon butter.

SWEET AND SOUR BEEF CASSEROLE

3/4 lb. stewing beef, cut in 1-in. cubes	1/2 green pepper, sliced
1 tbs. oil	3/4 cup button mushrooms, sliced
1/4 cup seasoned cornstarch	
2 tbs. honey	4 prunes, soaked
2 tbs. vinegar	2 tbs. green olives, stoned
3/4 pt. water	

Preheat the oven to 180 °C, 350 °F. Melt the oil in a 2½-pt. freezer-to-tableware saucepan or casserole and gently fry the beef until the cubes are browned on all sides. Stir in the honey, vinegar, and water. The add the cornstarch, blended with water.

Place the pan in the preheated oven and cook for 2 hr. After 1½ hr. add the carrots, prunes, and olives.

Cool the dish completely and skim off the fat. Cover with a lid and seal with freezer tape. Return to the oven for 45 min.

4 servings

TURKEY OR CHICKEN TARTLETS

1 onion, finely chopped	2 cups cooked, chopped turkey *or* chicken
2 tbs. butter	
1 15-oz. can apricot halves	1/2 tsp. Tabasco sauce
2 tsp. curry paste	Seasoning to taste
	4 oz. frozen peas
2 tsp. lemon juice	10 oz. Shortcrust Pastry
5/8 cup sour cream	Beaten egg to glaze

Cook the onion in butter until golden. Add the apricot halves. Simmer for 20 min., until reduced to a thick pulp. Thin the curry paste with a little water and add to the apricots with lemon juice. Stir in the sour cream and chopped turkey pieces. Bring to a boil and simmer gently for 10 min. Add the Tabasco sauce, and season to taste. Remove from heat and stir in the peas. Leave covered, to cool.

Make up the pastry in the usual way. Halve the dough and roll out ½. Cut out 5-in. rounds to line large individual pie pans. Divide the cooled turkey filling equally between the tarts. Using the remaining pastry, cut out and cover the tarts, glazing with beaten egg to make the edges stick. Pinch the edges together with thumb and forefinger and decorate the tops with pastry "leaves." Glaze with beaten egg. Cook for 15-20 min. at 220 °C, 425 °F, or until golden brown. To serve hot, heat at 180 °C, 350 °F, for 15 min. Cover with waxed paper before heating.

Supper Parties

SUPPER "BEFORE A SHOW"

Pre-theatre and other early evening suppers should be easy and quick to eat. They are intended to sustain one until later in the evening, rather than to be the final meal of the day, since time is usually a factor for people going to a show, concert, skating session, or other activity.

MINESTRONE

¾ cup kidney beans	2 carrots
2 qt water	1 small turnip
2 onions	2 sticks of celery
1-2 cloves of garlic	2 small potatoes
1 oz. lean bacon scraps	½ small cabbage
2 tbs. olive oil	⅓ cup macaroni or fancy shapes of Italian pasta
A bunch of herbs	Salt and pepper
2 large tomatoes	Grated cheese
½ cup red wine	

Soak the beans overnight in ½ pt. of the water. Slice the onions, crush the garlic, and chop the bacon. Heat the oil in a deep pan and fry the onion very gently for 10 min. Add the garlic, bacon, herbs, cut-up tomatoes, and the wine. Reduce this mixture by rapid boiling for 5 min. Add the kidney beans and the rest of water and simmer for 2 hr. Dice the carrots, turnip, and celery and add them to the soup; simmer for another ½ hr. Add the potatoes, diced, and simmer for ½ hr. more. Add the shredded cabbage and the macaroni and simmer for a final 10-15 min. Season the soup, stir a little grated cheese into it and pass the rest around separately.

Different mixtures of vegetables may be used when they are in season.

6 servings

SHRIMP PROVENÇALE

8 oz. frozen *or* fresh shrimps (weight when peeled)	2 tomatoes
	2-3 large mushrooms
	Seasoning
2 tbs. butter	2 tsp. chopped parsley
1-2 tbs. olive oil	Lemon juice
1 small onion	
½ clove garlic	

Separate frozen shrimps. Heat the butter and oil together, then fry the thinly sliced onion and the crushed clove of garlic (½ clove is sufficient for most people). Skin

Boston Baked Beans

Minestrone

and slice the tomatoes, slice the mushrooms and add to the onion with the shrimps and fry together until just tender. Season well, then add the parsley and lemon juice and serve at once.

For a more substantial dish serve on a bed of boiled rice.

2 - 3 servings

DEVILED CHICKEN LIVERS

4 chicken livers	Pinch of salt
1 shallot *or*	8 small strips
small onion	of bacon
½ tsp. chopped	4 Croutes of
parsley	fried bread
Pinch of cayenne	
pepper	

Wash and dry the livers; cut them in halves. Finely chop the shallot or onion

and mix with the parsley, cayenne papper, and salt. Sprinkle this mixture over the livers. Wrap the strips of bacon around the livers, and fasten them in position with skewers. Bake in a moderate oven (180 °C, 350 °F) for 7-8 min., or cook under the broiler. Remove the skewers, put 2 bacon rolls on each Croute, and serve as hot as possible.

4 servings

EGGPLANT WITH POACHED EGGS

3 eggplants	1 tbs. bread
1 tbs. butter	crumbs
⅝ cup tomato	Salt and pepper
pulp	6 small poached
2 tbs. chopped	eggs
ham	Chopped parsley

91

Boil the eggplants in slightly salted water until tender, or steam them. Halve them lengthwise, and remove seeds if necessary. Heat the butter, add the tomato pulp, ham, and bread crumbs, and stir over heat. Season well, then fill the cavities of the eggplants with the mixture. Put into a greased dish in a moderate oven (180 °C, 350 °F) and heat thoroughly. Place a poached egg on each half; garnish with parsley and serve.

6 servings   Cooking time – about 1 hr. altogether

RISOTTO

⅝ cup long-grain rice	2 tbs. grated Parmesan cheese
1 small onion	
¼ cup butter	2½ cups vegetable stock or water
Salt and pepper	

Wash and dry the rice thoroughly. Chop the onion finely; heat the butter and fry the onion until lightly browned. Then add the rice and fry it until brown. Put in the stock or water, add salt and pepper to taste, boil rapidly for 10 min., and afterward simmer slowly until the rice has absorbed all the liquid. Stir in the cheese, add more seasoning if necessary, then serve.

Alternatively:

1¼ cups long-grain rice	¼ tsp. pepper
¼ cup butter	Stock
1 small onion, finely chopped	2½ cups tomato sauce
½ tsp. saffron	½ cup grated Parmesan cheese
Nutmeg	
1 tsp. salt	

Wash, drain, and dry the rice thoroughly in a clean cloth. Heat the butter in a saucepan, put in the onion, and, when lightly browned, add the rice and shake the pan over the heat for about 10 min. Then sprinkle in the saffron, a good pinch of nutmeg, salt, and pepper. Cover with stock, and cook gently for about 1 hr., meanwhile adding the tomato sauce and as much stock as the rice will absorb, the sauce being added when the rice is about half cooked. Just before serving, stir in the cheese.

This savory rice is frequently used for borders instead of plainly boiled rice or mashed potatoes.

Either of these recipes can be used as a main dish, accompanied by small bowls of chutney, cooked shrimps, shredded green peppers, or canned red pimientos, sliced hard-boiled eggs, and other hors-d'oeuvre or salad ingredients. Each person can then choose the garnishes he prefers.

2- 3 servings

PEARS FILLED WITH NUT AND DATE SALAD

3 ripe dessert *or* canned pears	⅓ cup chopped walnuts
1 small head crisp lettuce	Chopped parsley
	French Dressing *or* salad dressing
¾ cup chopped dates	

Peel and halve the pears. Remove the cores with a sharp teaspoon, then scoop out a little of the pulp of the pears to leave a hollow for the filling. Shred a few lettuce leaves very finely and mix with dates, walnuts, chopped parsley, and finely diced pear pulp and French Dressing *or* salad dressing. Place the halved pears on small crisp lettuce leaves on individual plates. Pile the mixture on each piece of pear. If fresh pears are used, squeeze lemon juice over them to prevent discoloration.

6 servings

WAFFLES

2 cups flour	¼ cup margarine
¼ tsp. salt	2-3 eggs
1½ tbs. yeast	Maple or corn syrup
½ tsp. sugar	
2½ cups milk	

Sift flour and salt into a bowl. Cream the yeast with the sugar and add to it the warm milk and margarine; beat the eggs. Add the yeast, milk, and egg to the flour, using more milk if required to make a pouring batter. Set aside to rise for 30-45 min. Heat and grease the waffle iron and pour in enough batter to fill the iron sections — the lid must press on the batter. The waffles are ready when nicely browned. Serve hot with maple or ordinary syrup.

30- 40 waffles

APPLE-RAISIN LATTICE TART

Shortcrust Pastry, frozen *or* using 2 cups flour, etc.	½-¾ cup sugar, brown *or* white
	2 tbs. flour
1 tart dessert apple	Pinch of salt
	2 tbs. butter
1½ cups seedless raisins	
1 tbs. lemon juice	

Line a 9-in. pie plate with ⅔ pastry, reserving the rest for lattice strips. Peel, core, and chop apples, and toss in lemon juice to coat. Mix the fruits, and then mix in any dry ingredients. Turn into the pastry-lined plate. Dot with butter and arrange a lattice of pastry strips over the top. Bake in a very hot oven (230 °C, 450 °F) for 7-8 min., then reduce heat to moderate (180 °C, 350 °F) for 30-40 min.

LATE-NIGHT PARTIES

A late supper tends to be informal. The food should never be elaborate; it should be a dish that cooks "by itself" long and slowly, or is ready beforehand, or one that is easy and quick for the hostess to prepare.

FRENCH ONION SOUP

2 oz. bacon	⅝ cup white wine
6 medium-sized onions	
	6 small slices of French bread
2 tbs. flour	
Salt and pepper	
½ tsp. French mustard	2 oz. Gruyère *or* Parmesan cheese
3¾ cups stock	A little butter

Chop the bacon and heat it gently in a deep pan until the fat runs freely. Slice the onions thinly and fry them slowly in the bacon fat until golden. Add the flour, salt, and pepper to taste and continue frying for a few min. Stir in the mustard, the stock, and the wine. Simmer until the onions are quite soft. Toast the bread; grate the cheese. Butter the toast and spread the slices with grated cheese. Pour the soup into individual fireproof soup bowls, float a round of toast on each, and brown it in a very hot oven or under the broiler.

This soup can be served either at the beginning or end of a late-night party.

6 servings

FRIED SHRIMPS WITH TARTARE SAUCE

8 oz. frozen *or* fresh shrimps (weight when peeled)	Tartare Sauce
	Batter for coating (*see* below)
Fat for frying	

Separate the frozen shrimps or dry the fresh ones. Make the batter. Season well. Dip each shrimp in batter and lower into really hot fat. Cook quickly until golden brown. Drain on crumpled or absorbent kitchen paper. Serve on a hot dish with tartare sauce and serve a plain salad with them.

3- 4 servings

Batter for coating:

1 cup plain flour	1 egg
	⅝ cup milk
Pinch each of sugar and salt	

Sift together the flour and salt. Make a well in the center of the flour and add the egg and some of the milk. Mix to a stiff consistency, using more milk if required. Beat well. Add the rest of the milk. Let stand for about 30 min.

Eggplant with Poached Eggs

Waffles with fruit and jam

Pears Filled with Nut and Date Salad

French Onion Soup

TARTARE SAUCE

⅝ cup mayonnaise	A little French mustard
1 tsp. each of chopped gherkin, chopped olives, chopped capers, chopped parsley, chopped chives	2 tsp. wine vinegar A little dry white wine (optional)

Mix the chopped ingredients into the mayonnaise; add the mustard. Thin to the required consistency with the vinegar and wine.

BOSTON BAKED BEANS

1 lb. dried pea beans	4 tbs. blackstrap molasses
2 medium onions, peeled and thinly sliced	2 tsp. dry mustard
½-¾ lb. salt pork cut into 1-in. cubes	1 tsp. salt Good shake pepper

Wash the beans, cover with water, and leave to soak overnight. Drain but keep ½ pt. water. Fill a large heat-proof casserole (or traditional bean pot) with beans, onions, and pork. Combine the reserved water with the remaining ingredients, pour into casserole, then cover with lid. Cook in the center of a very slow oven (140 °C, 290 °F) for 5-6 hr. Stir occasionally and add a little more water if beans seem to dry slightly while cooking.

4 servings

SAVORY OMELETS

There are two types of omelet: the French, which is flat and generally served folded into thirds; and the English, which is fluffy and more like a soufflé. The essentials in making either type are a thick, clean, dry omelet pan of the right size, i.e. 6-7 in. in diameter for a 2- or 3-egg omelet; butter; eggs; and seasonings.

FRENCH OMELET

2-3 eggs Salt and pepper	1 tbs. butter

Break the eggs into a bowl. Add salt and pepper to taste. Beat the eggs with a fork until lightly mixed. Heat the butter in the pan and slowly let it get hot, but not so hot that the butter browns. Without drawing the pan off the heat, pour in the egg mixture. It will cover the pan and start cooking at once.

Shake the pan and stir the eggs with a fork, away from the side to the middle. Shake again. In about 1 min. the omelet will be soft but no longer runny. Let it stand for 4 or 5 sec. for the bottom to brown slightly. Then remove from the heat.

Using a spatula, fold the omelet from two sides over the middle. Then slip onto a hot dish, or turn it upside down onto the dish.

This omelet can be eaten plain, or it can be filled. There are two methods of filling: flavoring such as herbs or cheese can be added to the eggs after they are beaten, or added to the omelet just before it is folded.

Suggested savory fillings (quantities given are for 2-egg omelet)

Cheese Grate 2 oz. hard cheese finely. Add most of it to the mixed eggs, saving a little to top the finished omelet.

Fines Herbes Finely chop 1 tbs. parsley and a few chives, and add this to the mixed eggs before cooking.

Onion Sauté a large onion in a little butter but do not get it too greasy. When cool, add to the egg mixture, saving a few hot morsels for garnishing the omelet.

Kidney Peel, core, and cut 2 lamb's kidneys into small pieces, and sauté them in a little butter with a small chopped onion or shallot. Pile this mixture along the center of the omelet after cooking but before folding.

Mushroom Wash and chop 2 oz. mushrooms; sauté them in a little butter until tender. Put them along the center of the cooked omelet.

Shellfish Shrimps, prawns, crayfish, lobster, or crab, fresh or canned, can be used. Chop if necessary and warm slowly through in a little white sauce so they are hot when the omelet is cooked. Then pile the mixture along the center.

Spanish Make a mixture of chopped ham, tomato, sweet pepper, a few raisins, 1 or 2 mushrooms, and sauté in a little butter or olive oil. Add this to the egg before cooking; serve this omelet flat.

ENGLISH OMELET

Separate the eggs. Add half an eggshell of water for each egg to the yolks; beat them with a wooden spoon until creamy. Beat the whites until they stay in the bowl when turned upside down. Gently fold the whites into the yolks. Have the butter ready in the pan as for the French Omelet. Pour in the egg mixture, and cook until it is golden brown on the underside. Then put the pan under the broiler and lightly brown the top. Fillings are usually spread over the cooked omelet. Now run a spatula around the edge of the pan. Fold the omelet over and slip it onto a hot dish.

WELSH RAREBIT

2 tbs. butter *or* margarine	A few drops of Worcestershire
1 level tbs. flour	sauce
5 tbs. milk *or* 3 tbs. milk and 2 tbs. ale *or* beer	1-1½ cups grated cheddar cheese
	Salt and pepper
1 tsp. mixed mustard	4 slices of buttered toast

Heat the fat in a pan and stir in the flour. Cook for several minutes, stirring well. Add the milk and stir well over the heat until a smooth thick mixture, then add the ale, mustard, Worcestershire sauce, cheese, and a good pinch of salt and pepper. Do not overcook the mixture or the cheese will become "oily." Spread on the slices of buttered toast and put under a hot grill until golden brown. Serve at once.

A large quantity of Welsh Rarebit mixture can be made and stored in the refrigerator to be used as required.

4 servings or 8 small savories

GRILLED KIDNEYS

6 kidneys	Croutes of fried
Oil *or* oiled butter	bread
Salt and pepper	

Garnish:
Maître d'Hôtel Butter *or* **bacon rolls**

Prepare the kidneys as directed in the preceding recipe and keep them open and flat with a skewer. Brush with oil or melted butter and season with salt and pepper. Broil quickly, cooking the cut side first and turning frequently. When ready, remove the skewer and serve on croutes of fried bread on a hot dish. The hollow in the center of the kidney can be filled with a small pat of Maître d'Hôtel Butter, or the dish can be served with rolls of bacon.

6 servings   Cooking time – 5- 8 min.

LEMON MERINGUE PIE

Rich Shortcrust Pastry, using 8 oz. flour, etc.

Filling:

2 eggs	2 level tsp.
8-oz. can sweetened condensed milk	cream of tartar
	1 lemon
¼ cup sugar	

Make the pastry and line an 8- or 9-in. pie plate. Prick with a fork, and bake in a hot oven (450 °F) for 12 min. or until lightly browned.

To make the filling Separate the egg yolks from the whites. Beat the yolks until thick and lemon-colored. Fold in the condensed milk, lemon rind, juice, and cream of tartar. Pour into the baked pie shell. Spread with meringue made from the egg whites and the sugar. Decorate lightly with cherries and angelica. Bake in a warm oven (100 °C, 200 °F) for ½-1 hr.

Coffee and Tea Parties

BASIC PLAIN SCONES

4 cups flour	4-6 tbs. lard *or*
½ tsp. salt	margarine

and

2 tsp. bicarbonate of soda and 4½ tsp. cream of tartar with 1¼ cups fresh milk

or

2 tsp. bicarbonate of soda and 2 tsp. cream of tartar with 1¼ cups sour *or* buttermilk

or

4-6 tsp. baking powder with 1¼ cups fresh milk

Sift flour and salt and lightly rub in the fat; sift in the raising agents and mix well. Add *all the milk at once* and mix *lightly* to a *spongy* dough. Knead very lightly to make the dough smooth and roll out ½-¾ in. thick. Cut out with a 2-in. cutter, brush with egg *or* milk if desired, and bake in a hot oven (220-230 °C, 425-450 °F). If you prefer, the dough can be divided into 4 and each piece formed into a round cake and marked into 6 with a knife.

24- 30 scones   Cooking time – about 10 min.

VARIATIONS OF BASIC RECIPE

Cheese Scones
Add 1-1½ cups grated cheese to the dry ingredients above. Cut out in finger shapes or squares.

Cheese Whirls
Add 1-1½ cups grated cheese to the basic recipe. Roll out dough into oblong shape. Spread with cheese and roll up like a Swiss Roll. Cut into slices and lay on greased baking sheets with the cut side uppermost. Brush with milk or egg. If any cheese is left over, sprinkle it on and bake the whirls in a hot oven (220-230 °C, 425-450 °F).

20- 24 scones   Cooking time – 10- 15 min.

Fruit Scones
Add ¼ cup sugar and ⅓-⅔ cup fruit (currants, raisins, etc.) to the basic recipe.

Griddle Scones
Add ⅓-½ cup currants; roll out ¼ in. thick, cut into 2½-in. rounds or triangles; cook on both sides on a moderately hot

A table set for the "traditional" English tea

griddle about 5 min., until nicely brown and edges dry. Cool in a towel.

Nut Scones
Add ⅜-¾ cup chopped nuts to the basic or to the whole wheat recipe.

Sweet Scones
Add ¼ cup sugar and, if liked, 1 egg.

Molasses Scones
Add 2 tbs. sugar, 1 tsp. ground cinnamon. 1 tsp. mixed spice, 2 tbs. blackstrap molasses. Put the molasses in with ⅔ of the milk, then add the rest as required.

Whole Wheat Scones
Use half whole wheat flour and half plain flour.

LARDY CAKE

1 lb. white bread dough that has risen once	¾ cup currants *or* raisins
¾ cup lard	A little spice, if liked
¾ cup granulated sugar or a little less	Sugar syrup to glaze

Roll out the dough on a floured board, and put on half the lard in dabs, to cover ⅔ of the surface, as in making flaky pastry. Sprinkle with the sugar, fruit, and spices to your taste. Fold the dough into rhirds, folding the unlarded piece over first. Turn to the right, and repeat the sugaring, larding, and folding. Turn to the right again,

99

and roll once more. Fold again. Roll, this time to fit a shallow baking pan about 12×7 in. Let rise in a warm place, and cover with a clean tea towel. Because of the sugar, it will take longer than usual, but need only rise half its height. This will take about ¾ hr.

Bake in the center of the oven at 200 °C, 400 °F, for about ¾ hr., until brown and crisp. When cooked (or before), brush with a thick sugar syrup to give a glistening top.

1) The cake looks better if you score the top with a sharp knife into diamond shapes before putting it to rise.

2) It is better eaten hot.

3) This is a traditional recipe, which used to be made on the day bread was baked, or from a piece of dough kept in a cold pantry until the next day.

BATH BUNS

1 lb. flour	Good tbs. yeast
½ tsp. salt	⅜ cup sugar
6 tbs. fat	2 eggs
(margarine and	1-1¼ cups
lard)	warm milk

Sugar Syrup Glaze:

1 tbs. water	2 ts. sugar

Mix salt with warmed flour and rub in fat. Mix in most of the sugar. Mix to a light dough with yeast creamed with remainder of sugar, egg, and milk. Let rise until double its size, then knead lightly. Divide into 24 pieces and shape each 3½-4 in. long and 1 in. wide. Place fairly close together (so they join in baking) on greased baking sheets and let stand 15 min. Bake in a hot oven (220 °C, 425 °F) 10-15 min. To make the glaze: boil together the water and sugar until slightly syrupy. Brush the buns immediately as they come from the oven so that the syrup dries on top of the buns.

Dredge thickly with sugar. Break buns apart before serving.

Note: ⅓ cup raisins and ¼ cup chopped peel can be worked into the dough after it has risen.

24 buns   Cooking time – 10- 15 min.

CHELSEA BUNS

2 cups sifted	1½ tbs. currants
flour	or raisins
¼ tsp. salt	2 tbs. chopped
2 tbs. lard or	candied peel
margarine	2 tbs. sugar
1 tbs. yeast	
⅝ cup warm	
milk	

Mix flour and salt, rub in fat, cream yeast and add to flour with warm milk. Beat well and let rise to double its size. Knead risen dough lightly and roll out in a square of about 10 in. Sprinkle with the fruit and sugar and roll up like a Swiss roll. Cut roll into 9 pieces and put cut side uppermost. Place buns in a greased 8-in. cake pan so that they will join together when cooked, and allow to stand until up to the top of the pan. Brush with milk or egg. Bake in a hot oven (220 °C, 425 °F) for 20-25 min. When cooked, glaze and dust with sugar like Bath Buns.

9 buns   Cooking time – 20- 25 min.

PLAIN BUNS or COOKIES
BASIC RECIPE

(Self-rising flour can be used for any of the following, in which case omit the rising agent.)

4 cups flour	3 tsp. baking
¼ tsp. salt	powder
½-1 cup	2 eggs
margarine	⅔-1 cup milk
or lard	or enough to
½ cup sugar	make a stiff
Flavorings as	consistency
below	

Sift flour and salt into bowl, cut in fat with round-bladed knife, then rub with fingertips until quite fine. Add sugar and baking powder. Mix with egg and milk to a stiff consistency. (The fork with which the buns are mixed should stand up in the mixture.) Divide into pieces and form into rocky heaps on a greased baking sheet. Bake in a hot oven (220 °C, 450 °F) until springy and browned.

24- 32 buns   Cooking time – 10- 15 min.

VARIATIONS OF BASIC RECIPE

Chocolate Buns
Add ¼-⅜ cup cocoa to the flour and 1 tsp. vanilla extract with the milk.

Coconut Buns
Mix in ¾ cup coconut with the sugar.

Ginger Buns
Add 2 small tsp. ground ginger to the flour and add ¾ cup chopped or grated crystallized ginger with the sugar.

Lemon Buns
Add 1 tsp. lemon extract with the milk. Turn mixture onto floured board and make into a roll. Divide into 24 pieces, form into balls, brush with egg or milk, and sprinkle with sugar.

London Buns
Add ½ cup chopped peel and 2 tsp grated lemon rind when adding the sugar and form mixture into balls as for Lemon Buns. Glaze and sprinkle with sugar. Place 2 pieces of lemon or orange peel on top of each bun.

Nut Buns
Add ¾ cup chopped nuts when adding the sugar.

Raspberry Buns
Form basic mixture into 24 balls, make a hole in each bun, and place a little raspberry jam in the hole. Close the opening, brush with milk or egg, and sprinkle with sugar.

Rock Buns
Add ⅔-1 cup currants and ½ cup chopped peel when adding the sugar.

Seed Buns
Add 4 tsp. caraway seeds with the sugar.

SCOTTISH SHORTBREAD

2 cups flour	**½ cup butter**
¼ cup sugar	

Put the flour and sugar in a pile on a pastry board. Gradually knead the sugared flour into the butter with your hands. It is important not to let the butter become broken up. When a firm dough is formed, roll out, and shape into a cake about 1-in high. Decorate the edges by marking with a fork or fluting with finger and thumb, or make in a shortbread mold, and prick a pattern on top with a fork or skewer. Fasten a narrow band of paper around to keep the cake in shape. Bake in a warm oven (150-170 °C, 300-325 °F). Dredge with sugar when cooked.

Cooking time – about 1 hr.

SCANDINAVIAN TEA RING

1½ cups flour	**⅓-½ cup**
¼ tsp. salt	**warm milk**
1 tbs. sugar	**½-1 egg**
Small tbs. yeast	

Filling:

1½ tbs. ground	**Hot water to**
almonds	**mix to a**
2 tbs. sugar	**spreading**
	consistency

Icing:

¾ cup sifted	**Warm water**
confectioners'	**to mix**
sugar	

Decoration:

1½ tbs. blanched and chopped almonds

Mix flour and salt; add most of the sugar. Cream yeast with remainder of sugar, add warm milk and egg, and mix with flour to a light but workable dough. Let dough rise and, when well risen, roll out in an oblong shape. Spread with the almond mixture; dampen edges with water and roll up. Form into a ring or horseshoe shape; let set 10-15 min. Bake in a hot oven (220 °C, 425 °F), reducing the heat after 10 min. to fairly hot (190 °C, 375 °F). When cold, spread with icing and sprinkle with chopped almonds.

Cooking time – 20-30 min.

Orange Sandwich Cake

BASIC LARGE RICH CAKE
(A 7-in. CAKE)

¾ cup butter *or* margarine	Milk to mix
¾ cup sugar	⅛ tsp. salt
3 eggs	2 tsp. baking
2 cups flour	powder *or* other rising agents

Line a 7-in. cake pan with waxed paper or greased foil, or with silicone-treated paper. Cream the fat, add the sugar gradually, and beat until white and fluffy. Beat in the eggs, one at a time, making sure each is blended in thoroughly before adding the next. Sift in a little of the flour if the mixture shows any signs of curdling. Sift in the flour, salt, and baking powder gradually, and stir in lightly with a spoon. Add enough milk to make a fairly soft batter. Turn into the cake pan and bake at 180 °C, 350 °F, for 1-1½ hr. or until the cake is springy and brown on top.

If you want to use any of the variations below containing dried fruit, add the eggs to the creamed mixture, alternately with the flour divided into 3 parts. Probably no

other liquid will be needed, and the cake will be close-textured enough to hold the fruit.

VARIATIONS OF BASIC RECIPE

Cherry Cake
Add ¾ cup chopped glacé cherries when adding the flour.

Fruit Cake
Add 1-1⅓ cups currants, raisins, or dates to basic mixture. Add eggs and flour alternately. Stir in fruit mixed with some of the flour *after* eggs have been added.

Ginger Cake
Sift ½ tsp. ground ginger with the flour, add ⅜-¾ cup coarsely chopped crystallized ginger with the flour.

Lemon Cake
Add the grated rind of 2 lemons with the flour. The cake can be iced, when cold, with Lemon Glacé Icing.

Madeira Cake
Add the grated rind of 1 lemon with the flour. Place 2 strips of candied citron peel on top of the cake when mixture has begun to set (after about 30 min.).

Seed Cake
Add 2 tsp. caraway seeds with the flour.

RICH CAKES — SMALL

Use the mixture on page 55 for all these small cakes and variations. It is repeated here for your convenience.

BASIC RECIPE

¼ cup butter *or* margarine	¾ cup self-rising flour *or*
¼ cup sugar	¾ cup plain
1 egg	flour and 1 tsp. baking powder
	Pinch of salt
	Water *or* milk as required

Beat the fat and sugar until creamy and white. Beat the egg and add gradually; beat well between each addition. Sift to-

Mocha Cookies

gether the flour, salt, and baking powder. Gently stir flour, etc., into creamed fat; add milk *or* water to make a soft dropping consistency (water is considered best). Half fill greased muffin pans with the mixture and bake in a fairly hot to moderate oven (180-190 °C, 350-375 °F).

Note: This mixture may be baked in paper cupcake holders and decorated with glacé incing or cherries.

10- 12 cakes ' Cooking time – 15- 20 min.

VARIATIONS OF BASIC RECIPE

Cherry Cakes
Add ¼-⅓ cup coarsely chopped glacé cherries with the flour.

Chocolate Cakes
Sift 2 tbs. cocoa with the flour, and add a few drops of vanilla extract with the water or milk. The cakes may be iced with Chocolate Icing.

Coconut Cakes
Add 1½ tbs. coconut with the flour and add ¼ tsp. vanilla extract with the milk or water.

Lemon Cakes
Add the grated rind of 1 lemon with the flour, and ice with Lemon Icing.

Madeleines
Bake the basic mixture in greased dariole molds. Turn out when baked; cool. Spread all around top and sides with warmed apricot jam. Roll in coconut; decorate with ½ glacé cherry.

Nut Cakes
Add ¼-⅓ cup coarsely chopped walnuts, almonds, etc., with the flour.

Queen Cakes
Add ¼-⅓ cup currants *or* raisins with the flour, or a few currants may be placed in the bottom of each queen cake pan and the mixture placed on top.

VICTORIA SANDWICH

½ cup butter or margarine	1 cup flour
½ cup sugar	Pinch of salt
2 eggs	1½ tsp. baking powder

Cream fat and sugar very thoroughly. Add well-beaten eggs gradually, beating well between each addition — if sign of curdling, add some flour. Sift flour, salt, and baking powder and stir lightly into the creamed fat and eggs. Mix to a soft dropping consistency, adding a little water if necessary. Place the mixture in a prepared 7-in. baking pan and bake in a moderate oven (180 °C, 350 °F).

Cooking time – 40- 45 min.

DUNDEE CAKE

⅞ cup butter or margarine	3-4 eggs
⅞ cups sugar	1 level tsp. baking powder
3 cups flour	Milk or water
¼ tsp. salt	as required
2¼-3 cups mixed fruit — currants, raisins	Blanched almonds

Line a 7-8 in. cake pan with waxed paper. Cream the fat and sugar until light. Sift together flour and salt and mix the fruit with a small amount of the flour. Add the eggs and flour alternately to the creamed fat, beating well between each addition. Mix baking powder with the last lot of flour, stir in the fruit, and if necessary add a little milk or water to make a heavy dropping consistency. Put into the cake pan, make a slight depression in the center, and spread some split blanched almonds over the surface. Bake in a moderate oven (180 °C, 350 °F); reduce heat after ¾ hr. to warm to cool (150-170 °C, 300-325 °F).

Cooking time – 2½ hr.

LEMON OR ORANGE SANDWICH CAKE

1 Victoria Sandwich Cake	Crystallized lemon or orange slices
Lemon or orange-flavored Butter Icing	

Cut cake through the center and spread with flavored Butter Icing. Sandwich together again. Spread the top of the cake with icing, smooth with a knife, and finally decorate with slices of crystallized fruit.

A more pronounced flavor can be obtained by adding the finely grated rind of 1 lemon or orange when mixing the cake.

BASIC LARGE SPONGE CAKE

1 cup flour	½ cup sugar
Pinch of salt	Grated lemon
3 eggs	rind

Grease and flour a 6-in. cake pan with 1 tsp. flour and 1 tsp. sugar mixed together. Sift the flour and salt. Beat the eggs and sugar over a pan of hot water until thick and creamy. Fold flour, salt, and lemon lightly into the egg and turn the mixture into the pan. Bake in a warm oven (170 °C, 335 °F). When cold, split the sponge and spread with jam. Dust with confectioners' sugar.

Cooking time – 45 min.

MOCHA COOKIES

⅝ cup butter	1 tbs. liquid coffee
¼ cup sugar	Beaten egg
1¾ cups self-rising flour	
½ level tsp. powdered cinnamon	

Cream the butter and sugar together until light and fluffy. Sift the flour and cinnamon and add to the butter and sugar together with the coffee. Work together. Using a pastry bag and rosette cone, press out round and finger shapes on a greased baking sheet. Brush with beaten egg. Bake in a moderate oven (180 °C, 350 °F) for 25 min. or until golden brown.

BANBURY CAKES

Rough puff pastry using 2 cups flour, etc.; or puff or flaky pastry may be used

Filling:

2 tbs. butter	¾ cup currants
or margarine	2 tbs. chopped
2 tbs. flour	candied peel
¼ nutmeg (grated)	¼ cup brown
or ¼ tsp. ground	sugar
cinnamon	2 tbs. rum

Glaze:

Egg white	Granulated sugar

To make the filling: melt the fat, stir in the flour and spice, and cook for a min. or 2. Remove from the heat, add the fruit, sugar, and rum.

Roll the pastry out ¼ in. thick and cut into 3-in. rounds. Place a spoonful of filling in the center of each; dampen the edges and gather them together to form a ball; turn over so that the smooth side is uppermost. Roll each out and shape into an oval shape 4 by 2½ in.; make 3 cuts in the center. Put the cakes on a greased pan and bake in a hot oven (220 °C, 425 °F).

Brush with the egg white and dust immediately with sugar. Return to the oven for a few minutes, to frost the glaze.

14 cakes   Cooking time – 20 min.

CRUNCHIES

½ cup butter *or*	1 tbs. light
margarine	corn syrup
¼ cup sugar	1 cup rolled
	oats

Melt fat, sugar, and syrup in a saucepan and stir in the oats. Spread on a greased baking sheet with a raised edge, 7 by 13 in., to within ½ in. of the edge. Place in a moderate oven (180 °C, 350 °F) and bake until a good brown color and firm. Cut into fingers before completely cool.

16 crunchies   Cooking time – 20- 30 min.

SMALL ICED OR FRENCH CAKES

One oblong	Cake decorations:
Genoese pastry	chopped nuts,
cake, 1-1½ in.	crystallized
thick	violets, rose
Filling of your	petals, silver
choice: jam,	balls, glacé

lemon curd,	fruits, angelica,
Confectioners'	etc.
Custard *or*	Glacé icing
Butter Icing	

Cut the cake through the center, spread it thinly with filling, and join together again. If necessary, trim off the brown top of the cake, and brush off any loose crumbs. Cut the cake into rounds, triangles, squares, etc. Brush off loose crumbs carefully, and put the pieces of cake on an icing rack over a large flat dish.

Make the icing so that it will flow easily over the cakes but will not run right off. Pierce each cake in turn with a skewer, spear it, and dip it into the icing. Return it to the rack, and dislodge the skewer with a fork, so that you do not leave finger marks on the cake. Once or twice, you can change the color of the icing, say from white to pale pink to darker pink. Before the icing sets, arrange a little decoration on the top of each cake. When firm, serve the cakes in decorative paper cases.

About 24 cakes

VANILLA SLICES

Puff pastry,	A little glacé
using ¾ cup	icing
flour, etc.	

Filling:

1¼ cups milk	2 tbs. sugar
3 tbs. cornstarch	½ tsp. vanilla
2 egg yolks *or*	extract
1 whole egg	

Roll pastry ½ in. thick and cut into fingers 4 by 1 in. Bake in a fairly hot oven (220 °C, 425 °F) until pastry is well risen. Allow to cool.

Blend the cornstarch with the milk, beat in the egg yolks and sugar, and cook over a gentle heat until thick. Beat in the vanilla. Allow to cool.

Slit carefully through the center of the pastry fingers, spread the custard over one half, and sandwich the halves together again. Spread tops thinly with glacé icing.

8 slices   Cooking time – 20 min.

Coffee Walnut Cake

mond Paste. Spread the remaining 3 sides with glaze, roll up firmly, and join Almond Paste neatly. To decorate, pinch the 2 top edges between thumb and forefinger. Mark the top of the cake lattice fashion with a knife and decorate with cherries and angelica.

COFFEE WALNUT CAKE

½ cup margarine	1 cup self-
½ cup sugar	rising flour
2 eggs	⅜ cup chopped
1 tbs. liquid	walnuts
coffee	Coffee Icing

Cream together the margarine and sugar until light and fluffy. Gradually add the beaten eggs, beating well between additions. Stir in coffee and fold in sifted flour, together with chopped walnuts. Turn mixture into a deep 7-in. baking pan, well greased, and bake at 190 °C, 375 °F, for 25-30 min. Cool on a rack. Decorate with Coffee Icing and walnuts.

BATTENBURG CAKE

2 Victoria Sandwich Cakes made in oblong pans, 1 cake white and the other colored pink
1 tbs. Apricot Glaze
Almond Paste, using ⅝ cup ground almonds, etc.

Decoration:

Glacé cherries   Angelica

Cut the cake into strips 8-9 in. long and 1½ in. square at ends — 2 pink and 2 white pieces will be needed. Join these together with apricot glaze to make a block 9×3×3 in., with a pink and a white strip side by side, topped with a white and a pink strip, respectively.

Roll Almond Paste into an oblong, wide enough and long enough to wrap around the cake, leaving the ends open. Trim edges of Almond Paste. Spread top of cake with Apricot Glaze and invert onto Al-

Basic Recipes

These foundation recipes provide products used in many of the preceding dishes.

SHORT AND RICH SHORTCRUST PASTRY FOR PIES, TARTS, ETC.

FOR STANDARD SHORTCRUST PASTRY

2 cups flour	¼ cup lard
Pinch each of sugar and salt	Cold water to mix
¼ cup butter *or* margarine	

Sift the flour, sugar, and salt together. Cut the fats into the flour, using the fingertips or a pastry blender. Mix to a stiff paste with cold water.

FOR RICH SHORTCRUST PASTRY

2 cups flour	1 tsp. sugar
½-¾ cup butter (sweet type, if possible)	Cold water to mix (about 1 tbs.)

Make as above, on a flat surface rather than in a bowl. Before adding water, make a well in the dry ingredients, and put in the egg yolk. Sprinkle with the sugar, and mix with the fingertips or a knife. Add the water as required, and mix.

PÂTE SUCRÉE

2 cups flour	1 egg yolk
Pinch of salt	Cold water to mix
⅝ cup butter	
¼ cup sugar	

Sift together the flour and salt. Cut the butter into small pieces and rub it lightly into the flour, using the fingertips. Add the sugar and mix with egg yolk and sufficient cold water to make a stiff paste. Use as required.

In warm weather only a very small quantity of water will be required.

CRUMB PASTRY

Crumb pastry can provide a useful shortcut to making a tart shell or piecrust. It is made with bread crumbs, toast, cracker crumbs or cornflakes. The materials are crushed by hand, wrapped in a cloth and rolled with a rolling-pin, or are processed in an electric blender. As a rule, 3¾ cups crumbs combined with ⅜ cup melted butter are used, with sugar and spice flavoring to your taste. This should make a shell for an 8-in. pie plate or tart.

Mix the crumbs together with the butter well, and press firmly into the bottom and sides of the plate. Either chill, and then fill with a custard or firm fruit puree; or chill and then prick with a fork and bake at 180 °C, 350 °F, for 15 min.

Fatty crumbs may need less butter; stale whole wheat bread crumbs may need a little more. A luxury crust can be obtained by using Gingersnaps for the crumbs, or the following mixture:

1½ cups cracker crumbs	¼ cup thin cream
6 tbs. unblanched ground almonds	½ cup melted butter
	⅓ tsp. cinnamon

PUFF PASTRY

(For pies, tarts, tartlets, etc.)

4 cups flour	1 tsp. lemon juice
Pinch of salt	¾ cup cold water (approx.)
1 lb. butter	

Sift the flour and salt and cut in about 2 oz. of butter. Press the remaining butter firmly in a floured cloth to remove the moisture, and shape into a flat cake. Add the lemon juice to the flour and mix to a smooth dough with cold water. The consistency of the dough must be the same as that of the butter. Knead the dough well and roll it out into a strip a little wider than the butter and a little more than twice its length. Place the butter on one half of the pastry, fold the other half over, and press the edges together with the rolling pin to form a neat parcel. Leave in a cool place for 15 min. to allow the butter to harden.

Roll out into a long strip 3 times the original length but the original width, keeping the corners square and the sides straight to ensure an even thickness when the pastry is folded. Do not let the butter break through the dough. Fold the bottom third up and the top third down, press the edges together with a rolling pin, and half turn the pastry so that the folded edges are on the right and left. Roll and fold again and lay aside in a cool place for 15 min. Repeat this process until the pastry has been rolled out 6 times. The rolling should be done as evenly as possible and the pastry kept in a long narrow shape that, when folded, forms a square. Roll out as required and leave in a cool place before cooking.

Bake in a very hot oven (230 °C, 450 °F). The oven door should not be opened until the pastry has risen and become partly baked, as a current of cold air may cause the pastry to collapse.

BASIC BROWN SAUCE

1 small carrot	¼ cup flour
1 onion	2½ cups brown stock
2 tbs. drippings	Salt and pepper

Thinly slice the carrot and onion. Melt the drippings and in it slowly fry the onion and carrot until they are golden brown. Stir in the flour and fry it even more slowly until it is also golden brown. Stir in the stock, bring to simmering point, season, then simmer for ½ hr. Strain the sauce before use. Since frying the flour is a long process, extra color may be given to the sauce by adding a piece of brown onion skin, or a little gravy browning, or a little meat or vegetable extract, which will also add to the flavor.

Cooking time – 40 min.- 1 hr.

BASIC WHITE SAUCE

For a Coating Sauce:

¼ cup butter *or* margarine	2½ cups milk *or* stock (fish, meat, *or* vegetable to suit dish), *or* a mixture of stock and milk
½ cup flour	
Pinch of salt	

For a Pouring Sauce:

3 tbs. butter *or* margarine	2½ cups of liquid as for coating sauce
⅜ cup flour	
	Pinch of salt

Melt the fat in a deep saucepan, large enough to hold the amount of liquid with just enough room to spare for beating the sauce. Stir the flour into the fat and allow it to bubble for 2-3 min. over a gentle heat. On no account allow it to change color; this is a white roux. Remove from heat and stir in ½ the liquid gradually. Return to moderate heat and stir the sauce briskly until it thickens, then beat it vigorously. Season and use it at once. If the sauce must be kept hot, cover it with wet waxed paper and a lid, and, before use, beat it again in case skin or lumps have formed.

A **coating sauce** should coat the back of the wooden spoon used for stirring and should only just settle to its own level in the pan.

A **pouring sauce** should barely mask the spoon; it should flow freely and easily settle to its own level in the pan.

For melted butter sauce, beat in ¼ cup extra butter, a nut at a time, just before serving.
Cooking time – 15 min.

BÉCHAMEL SAUCE

2½ cups milk	6 peppercorns
1 small onion	A small bunch
1 small carrot	of herbs
2-in. celery stick	¼ cup butter
1 bay leaf	½ cup flour
1 clove	¼ cup cream
1 blade of mace	(optional)
Salt	

Warm the milk with the vegetables, herbs, salt, and spices, and bring it slowly to simmering point. Put a lid on the pan and stand it in a warm place on the oven to steep for ½ hr. Strain the milk, melt the butter, add the flour, and cook this roux for a few min. without browning it. Stir the flavored milk gradually into the roux. Bring the sauce to boiling point, stirring vigorously. For an extra smooth result, wring the sauce through damp muslin. If cream is used, add it to the sauce just at boiling point and do not reboil it.

Serve with chicken, veal, fish, or white vegetables.

Note: Béchamel Sauce may be made with ½ white stock and ½ milk; the result will have a good flavor but will not be so creamy in texture.
Cooking time – 40 min.

DEMI-GLACÉ SAUCE

1¼ cups Espagnole Sauce	⅝ cup juices from roast meat *or* ⅝ cup stock and 1 tsp. good beef extract *or* meat glaze

Boil the sauce and meat juices together until well-reduced. Skim off any fat before serving the sauce. Serve with meat, poultry, game, etc.

ESPAGNOLE SAUCE

1 onion	2½ cups brown stock
1 carrot	Bouquet Garni
⅜ cup mushrooms *or* mushroom pieces	6 peppercorns
	1 bay leaf
2 oz. lean raw ham *or* bacon	⅝ cup tomato pulp
	Salt
¼ cup butter *or* drippings	¼ cup sherry (optional)
½ cup flour	

Slice the vegetables; chop the ham. Melt the fat and fry the ham for a few minutes and then, very slowly, the vegetables until they are golden brown. Add the flour and continue frying very slowly until all is a rich brown. Add the stock, herbs, and spices and stir until the sauce simmers; simmer for ½ hr. Add the tomato pulp and simmer the sauce for another ½ hr. Wring the sauce through a tammy cloth or rub it through a fine hair or nylon sieve. Season, add the sherry, if used, and re-heat the sauce.

VELOUTÉ SAUCE

¼ cup butter	2½ cups good vegetable stock (*see above*)
6 button mushrooms *or* mushroom pieces	Salt and pepper

12 peppercorns	Lemon juice
A few parsley	³/₈-⅝ cup cream
stalks	
½ cup flour	

Melt the butter in a saucepan and gently cook the mushrooms, peppercorns, and parsley for 10 min. Add the flour and cook for a few minutes without browning it. Stir in the stock, bring the sauce to simmering point, and simmer for 1 hr. Wring the sauce through a tammy cloth or damp muslin. Season, add lemon juice, and reheat. Just at boiling point, stir in the cream. The mushrooms may be rinsed and used as garnish for the dish.

For fish dishes, use fish stock.

SUPREME SAUCE

1¼ cups Velouté	1-2 tbs. butter
Sauce	Nutmeg to taste
2 tbs.-¼ cup	Lemon juice
cream	Salt and pepper
1 egg yolk	

Heat the Velouté Sauce, preferably in a double boiler. Mix the egg yolk and cream, and stir into the sauce. Cook without boiling until the egg yolk thickens. Beat in the butter, a small pat at a time. Add a pinch of nutmeg, a few drops of lemon juice, season, and use the sauce at once.

TOMATO SAUCE

1 onion	2 tbs. cornstarch
1 small carrot	1¼ cups white
1 oz. ham scraps	stock or liquid
or ham bone	from canned
or rinds	or bottled
1 tbs. butter or	tomatoes
margarine	Salt and pepper
4 medium-sized	Lemon juice
tomatoes, fresh,	Sugar
bottled or canned	Grated nutmeg

Slice the onion and carrot. Put them into a saucepan with the ham and fry them in the fat without browning them for 10 min. Slice and add the tomatoes and cook them for 5 min. Sprinkle in the cornstarch; add the stock or juice; stir until the sauce boils. Simmer the sauce for 45 min. Rub the sauce through a hair or nylon sieve. Re-

heat, season, and add lemon juice, sugar, and nutmeg to taste.

ITALIAN SAUCE

1¼ cups Espagnole	¼ cup white
Sauce	wine (optional)
4 shallots	Parsley stalks
6 mushrooms	Sprig of thyme
1 tbs. olive oil	1 bay leaf
¼ cup stock	Salt and pepper

Chop the shallots and mushrooms and cook them very gently for 10 min. in the olive oil. Add the stock, wine (if used), herbs, and spices and simmer gently until reduced by half. Add the Espagnole Sauce and cook gently for 20 min. Season, and lift out the herbs.

PIQUANT SAUCE

1¼ cups brown	1 tbs. halved
sauce	capers
1 onion or	1 tbs. chopped
2 shallots	gherkins
3 tbs.	2 tsp. ketchup
mushrooms	½ tsp. sugar
1 bay leaf	(optional)
1 blade of mace	
2 tbs. vinegar	

Finely chop the onion or shallots; chop the mushrooms coarsely. Simmer the onion or shallots, the bay leaf and mace in the vinegar for 10 min. Add this mixture and the chopped mushrooms to the brown sauce and simmer until the mushrooms are soft. Add remaining ingredients. Do not strain the sauce but lift out bay leaf and mace. Serve with pork, lamb, or vegetables.

MAYONNAISE, HOMEMADE

1-2 egg yolks	Mixed vinegars
Salt and pepper	to taste — if
Mustard	posible, 4
⅝-1¼ cups best	parts wine,
olive oil	vinegar, or lemon
	juice; 2 parts
	tarragon; and
	1 part chili
	vinegar

The eggs and oil should be at the same temperature and not too cold. In summer it is easier to make a good mayonnaise beginning with 2 egg yolks.

Remove every trace of egg white from the yolks. Put the yolks in a thick bowl that will stand steady in spite of vigorous beating. Add to the egg yolks the pepper, salt, and mustard to taste. Drop by drop, add the olive oil, beating or whisking vigorously constantly. As the mayonnaise thickens, the olive oil can be poured in a thin, steady stream, but whisking must never slacken. When the mixture is really thick, a few drops of vinegar or lemon juice stirred in will thin it again. Continue whisking in the oil, alternately with a little vinegar, until the whole amount is added. If the mayonnaise should curdle, break a fresh egg yolk into a clean bowl and beat into this the curdled mixture just as the oil was added originally.

Various other ingredients are often added to mayonnaise to give a different flavor and color. They are useful when making a mixed hor-d'oeuvre or any other dish of mixed products coated with mayonnaise, for they identify the different ingredients and emphasize their variety.

Some variations are complex sauces in their own right. It is hardly worth making these for light savory dishes where, as a rule, only a small amount of each sauce is needed. So the following simple additions to plain Mayonnaise are suggested instead.

To ⅝ cup Mayonnaise, add:

1) 2 tbs. concentrated tomato puree and 1 sweet red pepper, chopped (Andalusian Sauce)

2) 1 tbs. cooked spinach puree and 2 tbs. light cream (Green Mousseline Sauce)

3) ½ tsp. horseradish cream, 1 tsp. each chopped parsley and chervil (Escoffier Sauce)

4) 1 tbs. yogurt (or sour cream), ½ tsp. chopped chives, and a few drops each of Worcestershire sauce and lemon juice (Gloucester Sauce)

5) ¼ cup mixed chopped fresh herbs, as many as you can get (Green Mayonnaise)

Savory Omelet with fish filling

An electric blender makes almost foolproof mayonnaise. Use a whole egg instead of yolks and 2 tbs. vinegar. Put these into the blender with the seasoning and blend at high speed for 10 seconds. Still blending, trickle in the oil gradually. The mixture will start to thicken after ⅝ cup has gone in, and will not "take" more than 1¼ cups.

White wine can be used instead of wine vinegar, and wine vinegar with a drop or two of Tabasco sauce can replace the chili vinegar.

FRENCH DRESSING

2-3 tbs. olive oil	1 tbs. wine vinegar
Pepper and salt	

Mix the oil and seasoning. Add the vinegar gradually, stirring constantly with a wooden spoon so that an emulsion is formed.

Alternatively, make the sauce in a bottle with a tight stopper. Keep it in the refrigerator, and shake vigorously before use. French Dressing will keep for several days if chilled. Lemon juice can be used in place of vinegar. Where suitable, orange or grapefruit juice can also be used.

A pinch of sugar, a little mustard, and 1 or 2 drops of Worcestershire sauce can be added.

VINAIGRETTE SAUCE

This consists of a simple French dressing to which the following are added:

1 tsp. finely chopped gherkin
½ tsp. finely chopped shallot *or* chives
½ tsp. finely chopped parsley
1 tsp. finely chopped capers
½ tsp. finely chopped tarragon and chervil (if available)

ASPIC JELLY

5 cups jellied veal stock	2 sticks of celery
¼ cup gelatin	2 egg whites
Bouquet Garni (parsley, thyme, bay leaf)	and shells ½ cup sherry (optional) ⅝ cup vinegar

Let the stock become quite cold, and remove every particle of fat. Put it into a stewpan with the gelatin herbs, celery cut into large pieces, the egg whites previously slightly beaten, and the shells previously washed and dried. Beat over heat until nearly boiling, then add the wine and vinegar. Then reduce the heat and simmer for about 10 min., strain till clear, and use.

MELBA SAUCE

To make Melba Sauce, pass the required quantity of fresh raspberries through a nylon sieve and sweeten with confectioners' sugar. The sauce is not cooked. Use as required.

MOCK MELBA SAUCE

2 tbs. arrowroot	5 tbs. raspberry jam
1¼ cups water	Juice of ½ lemon

Blend the arrowroot with a little of the water. Boil remaining water with the jam and lemon juice. Strain it on to the blended mixture, return to the pan, and boil, stirring all the time. Cool before using.

BEURRE MANIÉ

The most economical way to thicken gravies, sauces, and soups is with Beurre Manié or butter and flour kneaded together, usually in equal amounts. Work until smoothly blended, then drop small nuts of the mixture, one by one, into the near-boiling liquid. Beat the sauce until it boils, by which time the thickening should be smoothly blended in. Beurre Manié will keep for several weeks in a refrigerator.

SAVORY BUTTERS

General Method

Scald any herbs to be used, then chop all the ingredients. Crush and pound flavoring materials, or process in an electric blender. Cream butter, add the other items, and mix until fully blended. Vary the amounts to suit your taste. Sieve the mixture if a smooth butter is required for piping, rosettes, curls, etc.; or spread ¼-½ in. thick on a plate and chill until firm, then cut out in round pats with a pastry cutter, or shape into balls.

Use ¼ cup butter, and salt and pepper to taste, with the ingredients below.

Anchovy Butter 6 bottled anchovies, lemon juice to taste (use no salt).

Curry Butter ½ tsp. curry powder, ¼ tsp. lemon juice.

Deviled Butter ¼ tsp. each cayenne pepper, white pepper, curry powder, and ground ginger.

Garlic Butter 1-3 cloves blanched garlic, chopped parsley.

Herb Butter Good pinch each of dried thyme and parsley.

Lobster Butter 1 oz. lobster coral and spawn (raw if to be used in a sauce or soup).

Maître d'Hôtel Butter 2 tsp. finely chopped parsley, ½ tsp. each chopped chervil and tarragon (optional), ½ tsp. lemon juice. Spread on a plate and chill after making, cut out round pats, and use to top fish, steaks, etc.

Meunière or Noisette Butter Lemon juice. (Heat the butter until golden-fawn, colored, add the lemon juice, and use hot.)

Mustard Butter 1-2 tsp. French mustard.

Shrimp Butter ⅝ cup cooked, shelled shrimp, pounded; lemon juice.

Tarragon Butter 1 tsp. fresh tarragon, lemon juice.

Watercress Butter ¼ bunch finely chopped watercress.

GLAZES

To glaze is to make shiny. Pastry can be glazed with egg, sometimes called egg wash. Apricot or red currant glaze is used to brush over fruit tartlets, etc. Aspic Jelly is used on hors-d'oeuvres, cold fish dishes, etc., and Meat Glaze on both hot and cold meat dishes. Ham is sometimes glazed with syrup or jam. Icings such as Chocolate Glaze are used on cakes.

DEMI-GLAZE

Use clear stock suitable for consommé. Reduce it until slightly thick and "tacky."

GLAZE FOR MEAT DISHES, OR MEAT GLAZE

Strictly, you should reduce about 4 qt. clear stock to about ¼ pt. by continued boiling, uncovered. It is cheaper and quicker to add enough gelatin to strong stock to set it almost firm.

IMITATION MEAT GLAZE

Add 4 tbs. gelatin to ⅝ cup cold water. Warm gently, stirring until dissolved. Without boiling, add 1 level tsp. each of meat and yeast extract, and a little browning. Use hot to brush galantines, etc. Use soon; it does not keep well.

GLAZE FOR VEGETABLES

Make like Meat Glaze, using strong vegetable stock and yeast extract.

GLAZED VEGETABLES AS TRIMMINGS

Diced vegetables, slightly under- cooked	Butter *or* margarine
The cooking liquid	Granulated sugar

Drain the vegetables and put the cooking liquid into a saucepan. Melt the butter and sugar in it gently. Reduce if necessary, until there is just enough liquid to coat the vegetables. Add the vegetables, and toss. Simmer for a few min. until they are well coated and beginning to color.

GLAZES FOR PASTRY

1) Egg-wash or egg-white glaze. Brush pastry with well-beaten egg or slightly beaten egg white before baking. For a deeper color, use the yolk only, or the yolk and a little milk. Use for meat pies, patties, sausage rolls, etc.

2) Sugar glazes. Fruit tarts, flans, puffs, etc., can be brushed lightly with cold water and dredged with sugar just before baking. Sugar syrup can also be used. For a thin coat of icing, brush with beaten egg white and dredge with sugar when nearly baked, or use thin glacé icing after baking. Buns and plain cakes can also be glazed with egg white and fine or coarsely crushed sugar.

BOUQUET GARNI or BUNCH OF FRESH HERBS or FAGGOT OF HERBS

1 sprig of thyme	1 small bay leaf
1 sprig of marjoram	A few stalks of parsley
1 small sage leaf (optional)	A few chives (optional)
1 strip of lemon rind (optional)	Sprig of chervil (optional)

Tie all the herbs into a bunch with thick cotton or fine string. Alternatively, the herbs may be tied in a small square of muslin. Add to soups, stews, sauces, etc., while they cook.

PARSLEY AS GARNISH

Parsley is perhaps the commonest trimming or garnish for all kinds of savory dishes.

To blanch Bring a saucepan of water to a boil. Place the washed parsley sprigs in a strainer, dip it in the boiling water for a

MAKING A FLAN SHELL Read from left. 1, Lifting the pastry on a rolling pin. 2, Tucking pastry into flan case. 3, Filling the flan shell with beans. 4, Lifting the flan case off the baked pastry shell.

moment, then withdraw it and shake the parsley to dry it.

To chop Blanch the parsley so that it keeps its greenness and Vitamin C. Wring it in a cloth to dry it. Cut off the stalks, and chop finely with a sharp knife, using a downward, not a "sawing" stroke. Blanched parsley will not stain the chopping board.

To fry Immerse the washed and dried parsley in deep, hot fat for a few moments only.

CROUTES AND CROUTONS

A croute is a fried or toasted slice of bread (round, square, etc.) used as a base, usually for a savory item such as a roast game bird or a meat mixture. Many hors-d'oeuvres and snacks are served on small round croutes or fingers of bread. Croutes

are also used as a garnish for a rich dish such as a salmi, their crispness contrasting with the sauce.

Croutes should be cut from bread at least one day old, and should be ¼-½ in. thick.

To fry croutes

Use butter or oil, and make sure that the first side is crisp and golden before turning.

To make toasted croutes

Toast whole bread slices, and cut to shape after toasting, using a sharp knife.

TO MAKE CRESCENTS OR FLEURONS

Cut bread slices (or pastry) into circles with a pastry cutter. Then cut crescent-moon shapes from these, with the same or a slightly smaller cutter.

Index